George Campbell

The British empire

George Campbell

The British empire

ISBN/EAN: 9783337234027

Printed in Europe, USA, Canada, Australia, Japan

Cover: Foto ©Andreas Hilbeck / pixelio.de

More available books at **www.hansebooks.com**

BY
SIR GEORGE CAMPBELL, M.P.

CASSELL & COMPANY, LIMITED:
LONDON, PARIS, NEW YORK & MELBOURNE.

[ALL RIGHTS RESERVED.]

1887.

CONTENTS.

CHAPTER I.
INTRODUCTORY.
PAGE

Our Position compared to other Nations—Need to take Stock of the Empire—Baron Hubner—Drawbacks of Parliamentary System—Deficiency of Farmer-Colonists—Too great Haste to be Rich—Immense Variety of Races—Difficulties in Mixed Colonies—Localisation of Free Government—Possibility of Federation 1

CHAPTER II.
FREE SELF-GOVERNING COLONIES.

How far they are Part of the Empire—The Aborigines of these Colonies—Arguments for Federation—Advantages to Colonies of Present Position—Drawbacks of Position to Us—Diplomatic Difficulties—Difficulties in the way of Federation—Impossibility of Customs Union or Common Revenue—Arguments for Letting Alone so much as is Well—What is Really Necessary—Comparison of Great Britain with the Free Colonies—Colonial Federations *inter se*—Pressing Need of a United Diplomacy—How to Attain—Immigration to Free Colonies—Chinese, Pacific Islanders, and Indians—White Immigration—State-directed Colonisation—Free Trade in Population 10

CHAPTER III.
POSSESSIONS AND SETTLEMENTS NOT SELF-GOVERNING.

Situation compared to Free Colonies—Our Fitness for Enterprise in a Superior Capacity—But Difficulty of Controlling Adventurers—Our Resources, and the Danger of taking too much— Recent Extensions 36

CHAPTER IV.

INDIA.

Character of the People—And of our Rule—Our Military Forces—Armies of Native Princes—Affghanistan—Burmah; Political and Military Position there—Employment of Native Soldiers Abroad—Advantages of India to Us—Advantages to the Natives—Education and its Effects—The so-called Tribute—Our Rule a Paternal Despotism—Recent Demands for more Free Institutions—The Free Press and Free Speech—The Educated Natives—Local Government—Government of Native States—The Filling of Civil Offices—Effect of Use of English on those who have not that Language—Claims of Natives to Higher Offices—The Civil Service—The Indian Mahommedans—Their Position—Are they a Political Danger?—The Question of European Settlement in India—The Government of India and Parliament—Need of a Buffer 43

CHAPTER V.

CROWN COLONIES.

What Crown Colonies are—Unsatisfactory Position—Majority of Coloured Races—Former Self-Government of Whites—Recollections of Slavery—Importation of Labour—Forms of Government—Colonial Officials—Difficulty of Protecting Natives—Defiance of Free-Trade Principles—Oligarchy in Natal—Attempts to Establish a General Franchise—Comparison with Southern States in America—And with Cape Colony—Jamaica—Mauritius—British Guiana—Paternal Administrations ... 101

CHAPTER VI.

TERRITORIAL COMPANIES.

The North Borneo Company—The National African Company—Questions of Policy Involved 114

CONTENTS.

CHAPTER VII.

PROTECTORATES.

Variety of Forms—Protectorates in Africa—In the Malay Peninsula—In Oceania—New Guinea—Missionary Influences—Action of Traders and Adventurers—Trade in Arms—Trade in Strong Drinks 117

CHAPTER VIII.

RECAPITULATION OF CROWN COLONIES AND PROTECTORATES.

Size and Resources of these Territories—Cost to Britain—Ceylon, Straits Settlements, and Mauritius—West Indian Colonies—South African Colonies and Protectorates—The Basutos—The Zulus—Relations with Boer Republics—Bechuanaland—Temptations to Further Advance—West African Settlements—Borneo and New Guinea—Fiji—Hong-Kong and Port Hamilton—Mediterranean Possessions—Aden, Perim, and Socotra—Summary of these Possessions 129

CHAPTER IX.

IMMIGRATION TO TROPICAL TERRITORIES.

Under-Population and Over-Population—Importation of Labour from Africa—Immigration from India—Its Possibilities, Uses, and Abuses—Conditions Necessary to its Success—Chinese Immigration—The Polynesian Labour-Traffic—Naval Reprisals 150

CHAPTER X.

EXTENSION OR RETROGRESSION.

Limit of Room for Extension—Division of Ground with Germans and French—Question of turning over Native Races to Greater Colonies—Future of New Guinea—And of Pacific Islands—South Africa : a Compact South-Eastern Dominion there—Questions Involved in the Rule of Territories not Self-Governing 161

CHAPTER XI.

AFRICA.

Size and Character of African Continent—Our Position in South Africa and elsewhere—Suakim—Possessions of Foreign Powers —Character of the Interior and its Condition—Character of the People—Indian Empire forbids African Empire—Need of a Limit to our Possessions there—The Congo Treaty and State—Possible German, French, and Italian Extensions— Egypt, and our Position there 169

CHAPTER XII.

CONCLUSION.

Our Empire and our Duties—The Roads to India—The Politics of the Mediterranean—Of the Suez Canal—Of Egypt—And of Western Asia—Summary of the whole Empire 180

THE BRITISH EMPIRE.

CHAPTER I.

INTRODUCTORY.

I THINK there is no people whose lot one feels more inclined to envy than the Swiss. It is not only that they are comfortable and content in their own democratic way, but with no great wealth, moderate taxation, and a small revenue, more seems to be done for the people than elsewhere. In respect of roads and railways, they are behind none; nor in hospitals and other public institutions. In an efficient system of public education they are far ahead of us, and in most modern improvements—postal arrangements, telegraphs, and telephones, and all the rest of it —they seem (for popular use at any rate) to be ahead of almost any other people—certainly very far indeed ahead of us.

Compulsory military service, no doubt, they have, and handsome barracks are conspicuous; but these are mere militia depôts. The required periodical service is rendered in the immediate neighbourhood of their own villages, and, combined with constant popular rifle practice, suffices to make them very efficient soldiers for purely defensive purposes—a form of militarism which I believe to be by no means disadvantageous. It does not appear to detract from their industrial efficiency. Altogether, they seem happy in their own homes, and, when they are too crowded there, their character and their education make them welcome as earners and emigrants abroad.

Yet I would not attribute this happy result too exclusively to their position as a well-regulated federation of small self-governing communities in secure mountains, and free from the cares of empire. Something of the same kind may be seen in New England, and some other of the older States of the American Union, where a good distribution of the soil and local self-government by and for the people are combined with a share and active part in one of the greatest States in the world. The constitutions of the United States and of the component parts are more fixed than ours—they are, in a sense, much more conservative: their vast territory is all contiguous in one Continent, and their foreign anxieties are not great. In these respects they have a very advantageous position.

We are not so fortunate. At home it is our boast that our constitution is elastic; but it is an elasticity that gives no rest; it is always stretching, and never settled. Abroad our Empire is scattered all over the earth with no constitution in particular to bind it together. And, in spite of our enormous wealth and great revenue, so much seems to be absorbed by debts, and naval and military armaments, and wars, and operations, and complications of all kinds, that we are almost niggardly in expenditure for the benefit of our own people at home—compared to the Swiss, for instance; and while we spend vast sums on occasion of political excitement, we are timid in the extreme in regard to any comparatively small normal expenditure for Imperial purposes, which requires an annual parliamentary vote.

In truth, our Empire is attended with many cares and anxieties, alarms and troubles, and a heavy expenditure. Yet we cannot shake off these responsibilities if we would. Citizens of a great Empire we are and must be. But we are getting uneasy; we feel that things are not on an altogether safe footing; there is a disposition to examine, and see if improved arrangements are not possible. It is towards that examination that I seek to make a humble contribution.

As to qualification for such a task, I can only say that at various times I have seen something of Asia, Africa (North and South), America, and the countries of Eastern Europe—that I have had a somewhat exceptionally wide experience of different parts of India, and that for the last dozen years as a Member of Parliament, with no other avocations, I have both paid special attention to debates and blue-books, and have, during the recess, travelled very much, and taken notes of things political. I have never visited Australasia, and had some desire to go there, but it so happens that we have just had, from two most excellent pens, the result of such a tour—from Mr. Froude and Baron Hubner. The former may be suspected of some political proclivities, but the latter is certainly thoroughly impartial; so I am very well content to take vicariously a tour, which brings out all that could be learned by a mere traveller much better than I could do it. Baron Hubner is certainly a wonderfully acute observer, and much that follows has reference to a recent perusal of his "Through the British Empire."

Besides the very scattered position and miscellaneous character of the British dominions we labour under some special disadvantages for the management of a great Empire. First and chiefest is our parliamentary system. All free countries must be at a disadvantage in the management of dominions beyond the seas, but we are in some respects especially so. To a great extent this has always been felt. Our extreme party system, under which it is the everlasting function of the outs to find fault with everything that is done by the ins, drives our public men to study the parliamentary game, rather than to do boldly and continuously what is right. And the congestion of Parliament resulting from the attempt to concentrate both the domestic affairs of a great country—or perhaps it would be more correct to say three or four countries—and also the affairs of a great Empire in one chamber, is an evil which has long been growing. It has come to a crisis since I have been in Parliament. The Irish Parliamentary difficulty has brought things to that pass that the aim and object of all Ministerial tactics is by hook or by crook to avoid all inconvenient discussions, and get the most necessary work through in some way or other. In no department is this more manifest than in that charged with our Colonial relations. There never was much method in our Colonial system; we have always managed from hand to mouth, as it were, in the case of each Colony; but of late there seems to be such a dread of troublesome questions that there is one settled purpose of a negative character, and that is to get rid of everything involving responsibility as much as possible, by every means to cast responsibility on some one beyond the ocean, to keep it out of parliamentary atmosphere. This has not only taken the shape of the most liberal concessions of self-government, but also in more recent times of attempts to shift the management of unfree dependencies and the relations with uncivilised tribes on to the shoulders of self-governing Colonies. That involves great questions, which I will come to later.

Another difficulty is of quite another kind, and one not generally realised, but, nevertheless, I think a very practical difficulty. I mean the character of British colonists. Owing to our modern system of agriculture we produce, but very little, the true colonist, in the proper sense of the word, the man who is content to settle down as a farmer, working with his hands and laboriously to develop new countries. Our own farmers are now employers of labour, not hand-workers, and neither their sons nor those of other classes above mere labourers much care to come down to hand labour. Those who have the energy to go abroad want to become traders and speculators and employers of labour rather than small farmers. Farm labourers and artisans of all sorts have not the capital and the aptitude to start as small farmers. When we look to the Irish small farmers and Highland crofters we find that they again are for the most part in too low a grade of farming to take to that trade successfully in new Colonies without special assistance. It is notorious that the Irish emigrants mostly take to day labour and not to farming. The Ulster men, called Scotch-Irish, and a few Scotch, are almost the only Britishers who are at all prominent in that way. Wherever you go in America you find most of the successful farmers to be Americans, Germans, Scandinavians, and other races —anything but Britishers—the Scotch, Scotch-Irish, and Ontario men excepted. All over the world the tendency is too much for the British to divide themselves into employers of labour and labourers, rather than independent colonists.

Then, trading country as we are, it is very natural that a large proportion of British fortune-seekers should be traders. But more than that, we have been demoralised by the prosperity of the last fifty years. Those of us who have lived so long can well remember the innumerable instances in which from small beginnings fortunes have been made – the evidences of wealth and luxury are all around us. Hence, among all who are enterprising and conscious of their powers, there is now too great haste to be rich; an idea that wealth is to be obtained by short cuts, a disposition to speculation and high-pressure advance, which will not be satisfied with common hard-working gradual advance. This disposition is shared to the full by the numerous joint-stock companies which seek to explore new lands. Such a boom as we have had in the last generation is not likely to recur, but it influences the spirit of the age.

To these causes it is due that wherever there is a British Colony, or wherever British adventure penetrates, there is land-jobbing. In these days of immense railroad extensions and great developments the United States have not been free from land-jobbing. The great concessions to railways and other enterprises have given opportunities for the acquisition of great tracts by capitalists, and the homestead laws have been much evaded and abused. But for several generations the Americans, wisely I think, set themselves very strongly against the accumulation of land in few hands, and insisted on the very wide distribution of homesteads. Hence it is that, recent developments apart, the States are in the main a land of small farmers. And even where colossal properties have been acquired, the set of habit and public opinion is such that the proprietors rather look to profit by selling to farmers than to maintain great estates. A large proportion of the rented farms are those of Africans in the southern States. It is otherwise in British Colonies. The older Canadian provinces were settled on American principles, but in Manitoba and the North-West land speculation largely prevails— the most accessible lands are taken up before the true colonist arrives. Mr. Froude and Baron Hubner both entirely agree in exposing and denouncing the extent to which, in the Australasian colony most fitted for colonisation and agriculture, New Zealand, land monopoly has been carried. And in the greater part of Australia proper, free selection and all the rest of it notwithstanding, it would seem that most of the land is in the hands of big men. Despite a certain proportion of genuine farmers, society there is too much divided into plutocrats and labourers for high wages claiming monopoly and protection. Even the great landholders are now surpassed by the great land-speculators. As Baron Hubner puts it: "The principal source of the large fortunes which have been and are still being made lies in the sale and purchase of land. There are men who make a trade of it, and sometimes amass colossal wealth." And again, referring to the cry for extensions in the Western Pacific and elsewhere, he quotes one of his informants as saying: "It is a craze which is accounted for by the wants of speculators continually in quest of lands to buy and sell."

In the case again of our traders in search of new markets and rapid riches, our Consuls say that they study foreign tastes and manners too little, and trust to political influences and gunboats too much. Pushing and successful pioneers and bold energetic adventurers we are. But all this energy and push make it the more difficult for not very efficient offices at home to keep peace and order all over the world, to follow and, when necessary, restrain adventurous British subjects.

The greatest difficulty of all is, the immense variety of races of which the British Empire is composed. Even in the Colonies proper—the temperate regions settled by white men—we have not only great settlements mainly British, but also considerable territories acquired by conquest, and still possessed by French, Dutch, and other colonists; yet now so intertwined with British settlements that we could not get rid of them if we would.

Then in all our foreign possessions we have, more or less, the aboriginal races still subsisting—in the warmer countries we have them in great numbers. Most difficult of all are those Colonies in which we have at the same time white settlements, and a native population who cannot be despised. To reconcile the conflicting interests of these two classes is a very hard task. To white colonists we have conceded an ample self-government, which is, one may say, their birthright. In other territories, and especially in the great dominion of India, we have sought to govern by what may be called a benevolent despotism—a form of government which may indeed be very good for the progress and happiness of mankind, if we can ensure that the despotism is really benevolent and good, and the people are not so saturated with a love of independence as to revolt from an administration, however good, which is not their own. It is in countries where the white colonists claiming self-government are so numerous that their claims cannot be ignored; while the coloured people are a large and important population, that the form of government is so difficult to settle. Above all things it is desirable to avoid the risk that either what purports to be a crown government for the benefit of all, or free institutions conceded to a white minority, should in either case degenerate into an oligarchy—that is, the worst of all governments. I fear that in some of our Colonies the tendency is too much that way.

I think all history shows that free governments only succeed when the unit of government is small—when communes, self-governing in much, make up small States; and great free nations are only successful when they are composed of a federation of smaller States. Ancient Greece, and modern Switzerland and America, are examples, while too centralised France shows the evil of the opposite system. On consideration, we may well see why it should be so. When power rests with the people, we must take them as they are; they cannot all be political philosophers and diplomatists. The "vox populi," that is, the average consensus of many minds, will generally be the right thing in matters which the "populus" understands, in matters which they see and know, and in respect of which they can really judge what is good for their own and their neighbours' interests. But when we come to greater and wider matters, beyond the average ken of the elector, he cannot be expected to exercise a very independent judgment; he is too apt to be led by newspapers and politicians. The representative, too, whom he would choose to regulate his immediate domestic concerns, may not be the best to deal with larger matters. And if we attempt to deal with too much in one assembly, that leads to trouble, as we know to our cost. I have, then, long been a strong advocate for the decentralisation of the British legislature, and rejoice that, among all parties, the belief in the necessity for a re-arrangement of that kind is coming to the front. But I do not propose to enter on that here. I am rather dealing with Greater Britain, and I only mention the subject in this connection because it affects the question of Imperial administration in two ways: first, because, if a large part of our domestic affairs were relegated to local assemblies, we might hope to obtain a more efficient Imperial administration; and second, because the idea of a federated administration at home has, as it were, dove-tailed with the idea of a federal constitution to include the Colonies. This latter idea has of late begun to excite a good deal of attention—even, I may say, a good deal of enthusiasm with some people. Perhaps it would be too much to say that it has already received Imperial recognition, but, in cautious language, Her Majesty's Government have formally propounded the question whether some means may not be found of drawing closer the connection with our great self-governing Colonies. And so, in that shape at least, the question has come within the region of practical politics, and must be examined.

CHAPTER II.

FREE SELF-GOVERNING COLONIES.

BEFORE going to other questions I will then deal with the subject of our free self-governing Colonies. The first thing to be said of these Colonies is, that it is at present almost a misnomer to speak of them as part of the British Empire at all. We certainly do not exercise any real authority whatever over them, nor is there any common authority that does to any considerable extent—for in these days the golden link of the Crown is little more than a nominal and sentimental link. They are rather friendly allied States. They are complete and absolute masters of their own internal affairs, and will brook no interference. The Colonists being for the most part people of our own race and habits, prosperous and rich, and with few manufactures of their own, are very good customers for our goods, but in matters of commerce and trade they show us no favour whatever; on the contrary, they have established heavy protective duties in direct conflict with our free-trade system. Of late years the Governors—the constitutional vice-kings—have even ceased to be the sole channels of communication with the Colonies; the Colonial Governments have set up diplomatic agents in London, under the title of "Agents-General," who communicate direct with the British Ministry.

It has sometimes been thought that it would have been better if, following the example of the United States, we had made some reservations when self-government was granted to the Colonies; if we had, like the States, treated the great public lands as the domain of the nation and not of the early Colonists, made some stipulations for freedom of commerce, and protected the natives. If our system at headquarters had been very efficient, perhaps this might have been attempted with advantage; but, situated as we were, perhaps matters were arranged for the best. Whatever drawbacks there may be, the system has at least produced great contentment and a spirit of friendliness in the Colonies. It may not improbably be that under the Colonial Office land-jobbing would have been at least as rampant as under Colonial administration. We did attempt to reserve the management of the natives, but with singular want of success. As it is, in all the great Colonies where the natives are few and sparse, there is no longer a native question for us—we have made them completely over to the Colonial Governments, and if we interfere at all it can only be by the moral force of public opinion. In Canada we do not think of interfering in questions between the Canadian Government and half-breeds or Red Indians. From Australia come stories, with or without foundation, of occasions on which the wild aborigines are shot down like vermin or practically enslaved. But we can only join our own public opinion to the better public opinion of Australia to deprecate the possibility of such things; the interference of our Government is impossible.

In New Zealand, the Maoris had treaties with the British Government, reserving to them large rights and privileges, but these obligations have been transferred to the Colonists. In case of non-fulfilment we might have a ground for, and perhaps an obligation to, a sort of diplomatic remonstrance. But it may be doubted if it would have much practical effect, and whether, by rousing Colonial jealousies, we might not do the Maoris more harm than good. Baron Hubner is evidently very much inclined to doubt the maintenance of Maori privileges. According to him, the Colonial feeling in regard to the native reserves at present closed against the whites is, "At whatever cost, it must be opened to civilisation, to culture, and, above all, to speculation." And he sums up: "The white has nothing to fear from the Maori; the Maori has nothing to hope for from the white. There is no longer any Maori question." We must trust that this is a somewhat pessimist view, and that the Maori remnant will survive. But be that as it may, it may be really said that neither in Canada nor in the free Australasian Colonies, public opinion apart, is there any native question for us—we have made over the natives to the Colonists for weal or for woe. Only in Western Australia we may remember that the executive is still in the hands of the Crown, and we are so far responsible for the treatment of the aborigines there, regarding which there have lately been some unpleasant statements.

In South Africa the native question is in our hands only because there the natives have proved themselves too strong for the Colonists. We made over the native territories beyond the Kei to the Cape Government, but it was only by British regiments and British money that the dominion of the whites was established. And when the Colonists themselves tried to conquer the Basutos they were beaten, and obliged to render back that Trojan gift to the long-suffering British Government. The handful of Europeans in Natal wisely declined to avail themselves of the gift of complete self-government, coupled with the obligation to defend themselves. The native question in South Africa must be reserved till we come to the question of dealing with coloured races, in which it forms the most difficult problem.

To revert to the general question of the self-governing Colonies—while they are practically independent of us in most things, their connection with us involves to us several serious responsibilities and risks, and questions in regard to which no recognised and legitimised mode of solution has been provided. From our point of view, then, some federal arrangement under which these things might be provided for seems very tempting. But there are very great, perhaps insuperable, difficulties in the way of any large scheme of this kind. What strikes me forcibly is, that those who are almost enthusiasts in the matter, and have inquired into, and examined the question very anxiously— Mr. Froude, for instance—confess that they have been unable to see their way to any practical solution, or even to find any likely suggestions for its solution. The only suggestion that seems in some quarters to have taken a somewhat practical shape is, that the Colonies should contribute towards the cost of the British Navy in proportion as it is used for their defence. That seems in itself a very desirable arrangement, and voluntary contributions towards the great armaments for which we pay would be very welcome. But I confess I am a little suspicious. Whence this new-born zeal to pay for our armaments? If Colonists pay for a squadron of the British Navy, will they not want to have some control over that squadron? Self-defence is of all things most highly to be encouraged, but when, going beyond mere coast defence— floating batteries and stationary torpedo boats—Australian Colonists come in some sort to control sea-going vessels of war, whether their own flying the British Naval flag, or a squadron of the British Navy, may not the desire for such things be connected with the desire for acquisitions in the Pacific, beyond their own borders, at which some of them aim, and for a sort of independent foreign policy in those regions? That would raise very serious questions.

I confess that if I were a Colonist, apart from transmarine ambitions, such as those to which I have alluded, I should be very much inclined to let well alone. The

Colonists seem to have everything they can desire—most complete self-government at home; at the same time all the privileges and profits of the British Empire, and of all the British Services; the run of the London money market on the most favourable terms, and an immense influx of British capital; a full share of the honours bestowed by the Crown; a very welcome reception into British society for those who choose to bring back their wealth—a disposition, in fact, to pet Colonists in London, which may well be very pleasant to prosperous men after the troubles and the ups and downs of somewhat tempestuous and democratic Colonial situations. Then, in all difficulties, they have the whole force of the British Empire behind them; and in any questions which may arise with us they are pretty sure, under present conditions, to have the best of it. Baron Hubner makes even his optimist say, somewhat cynically, "We are strongly attached to the old country, but we are spoiled children, and our mother can refuse us nothing. When she seems about to thwart us we get angry. She then ends by giving way; and on these terms we shall always be well-behaved and affectionate children." I suspect there is much truth in that. The Baron instances the case of New Guinea. Queensland proclaimed the annexation of New Guinea; the annexation was annulled by the English Government. "Urgent requests made again and again were at first categorically refused by Lord Derby, then gently put aside, and ultimately admitted in principle. This fact," he goes on, "which is extremely significant, exemplifies the nature of the relations between the Colonies and the Imperial Government."

It has been suggested that the Colonies might suffer in case of the British Empire being involved in war. Let us look at that. There is one special case in which the risk cannot be palliated—the possible, though, we may hope, very improbable, case of war with the United States, in its effects on Canada. It is ten to one that, if such a war unhappily did occur, it would be on account of some Canadian quarrel. But, in any case, we must recognise that, great as Canada may look on our maps, and largely as its square miles may bulk in our statistics, habitable Canada is but, comparatively speaking, a strip, thousands of miles long, running along the frontier of the United States, without any natural boundary whatever in almost any part of this immense line. It seems hardly possible that in the event of war such a line could be throughout defended against the great power and great population of the United States; the line must inevitably be broken, the Canadian Pacific interrupted, and the Canadian Dominion cut into separate pieces. If Canada could not defend such a frontier with our assistance, still less could she do so without aid. One can only say that such contingencies are the inevitable result of the separate existence of Canada on the American continent. But in every other case of any other war with any other people, it seems hardly possible that any Power could send expeditions across the great intervening oceans that would very seriously affect the position of Canada or Australia. To say nothing of the British Navy, those countries are quite strong enough to defend themselves against any such expedition that could be thus sent out and might (very improbably) reach its destination. One can hardly imagine a Power at war with Britain expending its forces in such a way.

As regards the mercantile marine, the trade of the Colonies is chiefly British trade. It would be just as liable to interruption by a British war if the Colonies were independent. And, meantime, being British trade as well as Colonial trade, we are bound to protect it in our own interests, whether the Colonies assist us to do so or not.

On the whole, I think we may safely say that the

Colonies gain very much and are liable to lose very little by the present form of connection.

Besides these general considerations, the several self-governing Colonies have separate reasons of their own for loyalty to the British connection. Canada, during a hundred years of separation, has established a sort of national feeling adverse to the idea of being merged in the United States, to which may be added a certain commercial and industrial jealousy. Naturally, then, as she is situated, face to face, along all that long frontier, with a people more than ten times as numerous, and more than ten times as powerful, she clings to the support of the British connection. The French difficulty in Lower Canada has been happily settled by liberal Provincial self-government. Separated from France before modern France was created, the French Canadians have no proclivities towards France; they are content with the present situation. Altogether, then, the Americans frankly admit that the Canadians are loyal to Britain. As Baron Hubner puts it, "Their loyalty is based on interest, and is consequently firm and genuine."

I will not say more in this place of the desire of some of the Australasians to establish for themselves a kind of "Monroe doctrine" in the Pacific by the aid of the British power; but apart from that, we may say this—that the Australian Colonies are too young to have got up any separate national feeling; the Colonists are our brothers, and sons, and cousins, not only figuratively, but in the most literal sense. Several of our own present statesmen and Ministers have been Australasian Colonists at earlier periods of their lives. At this day it is the leading Australasians more than any other Colonists who find themselves at home in the Mother Country, and who appreciate the honours and attentions which are showered on them. However jealous, therefore, they be of their Colonial rights and privileges, and however possible it be that another day these distant Colonies may prefer independence, at present they have no serious aspirations of the kind.

In South Africa the position is different. The whites are there face to face with the black millions who press southwards from the interior of Africa. The Dutch of the Cape Colony, who have tasted the comfort and the profit both of British peace and British wars, might or might not be willing to risk independence and to make common cause with the Dutch beyond their borders. But the English of South Africa, in addition to anxiety about the natives, have a strong jealousy of Dutch ascendency; there is an English Imperial party just as there is in Ireland, and they are just as unwilling to submit to separation. They are afraid even of any Colonial federation which might give a preponderance to the Dutch element.

Altogether, then, so far as the Colonists are concerned, everywhere interest as well as sentiment very much tends to maintain the present connection with the British Empire; and it is always a question whether any large change might not be for the worse.

When we look at the question from a British standpoint, the matter is not quite so clear. Allusion has already been made to several disadvantages to us in present arrangements. The cost of all common concerns is borne by us. In questions between ourselves and the Colonists we are, as has been said, generally obliged to give way. More serious is the constant risk of complications with foreign Powers which results from the action or the susceptibilities of almost independent Colonies scattered over the world. Between Canada and the States there are those everlasting fishery questions, and other matters of comparatively small importance, which we might more easily settle if these affairs were our own, but in respect of which it is much more difficult to satisfy Canadians and

Newfoundlanders. At first sight one might have expected that Australia, divided from the whole world, would be free from such complications; but it is very much the contrary. Since the Australians have cast their eyes beyond their own shores, we have in those regions very burning foreign questions indeed. We know what a strong feeling there is in regard to French dealings with the New Hebrides, and Mr. Froude gave an alarming account of the dangerous state of excitement of Australians on the subject of German extensions. If, he says, the Australians had then had a sea-going fleet of their own, they might have brought about the most serious collision. His view seems to be that, on the part of the best men among the Colonists, the suggestion to substitute for war-ships of their own, the plan of a naval subsidiary force supplied by Britain, was designed to avert dangers of this kind. As Mr. Froude truly says, "No State can preserve its unity with two executives." Those are words to be seriously borne in mind. And then he adds, "As matters stood, the anger was directed as much at England as at Germany." There lies our peculiar difficulty: if the Colonists don't get their way, they blame us. It must be said that the same character of spoiled children, which leads them to expect the Mother Country to give way in questions affecting herself, also leads them to be somewhat exacting in questions between themselves and foreign Powers; and the difficulty is immensely enhanced by this—that their foreign relations and negotiations with foreign Powers are not in their own hands and on their own responsibility, but in those of a British Minister responsible to the British Parliament. They do not readily accept the decisions and the diplomatic bargains of a Minister not their own, when the arrangements do not wholly please them. The unfortunate British Minister must not only do the best he can in a give-and-take way, to come to terms with foreign Powers, but must

satisfy as well Colonists jealous and disposed to stand to
the utmost on their rights. As a matter of fact, we have
no means whatever of enforcing diplomatic decisions upon
self-governing Colonies who do not like them, as some
recent cases have shown. It is not long ago that, in a
comparatively small fishery dispute between Newfoundlanders and the United States fishermen, a certain compensation for damages was awarded to the latter, as part
of a settlement. But the Newfoundland Legislature flatly
refused to pay. All remonstrances were vain—there was
no getting out of the decision, and at the same time it could
not be enforced; so, as the only means of solving the
difficulty, a vote for the amount was smuggled through
the British Parliament late one night, at the fag end of the
Session—and the British taxpayer paid the money, for an
affair with which he had nothing on earth to do. It was
but a small matter, but it raises a very large question; the
same thing might occur on a much greater scale; something will have to be settled. Foreign affairs may involve
tremendous issues—great storms may come of small clouds.
One scarcely dares to allude to the gravity, one might
almost say the impossibility, of the situation if we had to
back Canada in a serious quarrel with the United States.
The *entente cordiale* with France is already sufficiently
strained without the added risk of Colonial quarrels. For
the present we seem to have settled most questions with
Germany by effusively offering to let the Germans have
what they want in Africa, and dividing the Pacific with
them into two happy hunting grounds; but there are still
burning questions in Samoa and elsewhere, in which the
Colonists take an interest, and questions between German and British adventurers may yet crop up in distant
parts.

No doubt, then, the idea of a great federated Empire on
the principle of the United States is a tempting one. Or

if not so much as that, there is great need of some mode of regulating common action. If there is to be one Empire, there cannot be in any part of the Empire two foreign policies, or two executives for Imperial purposes. For so much there must be supreme power somewhere.

But when we come to look more closely at the idea of an organised federation, the difficulties become immediately evident, and it has already been said that the most ardent advocates of the idea admit that they are unable to devise a practical plan.

In the first place, geography and mere distance stand in the way, and make impossible any union similar to that of the United States, who own the bulk of a great continent cut off from the rest of the world, and have for neighbours, north and south, only confederacies on a much smaller scale than themselves. They make it a fixed policy to accept no foreign possessions. Canada is separated from us by a great ocean, and its geographical and political position have been already dealt with. Australia is literally at the Antipodes, as far from us as is possible in this round globe. South Africa is both distant and has many complications, of which we will say more later.

Then there can be no doubt that the Anglo-Saxon spirit is localising and independent rather than centralising. We are proud of our country, but we look more to our immediate surroundings. British Colonies, small and great, have always had a tendency to claim and exercise a very complete control over their own affairs, and to resent interference. Even the man who has emigrated but a few years is often the loudest assertor of local rights and claims, and the most violent denouncer of a tyrannical British Government, in the making of which he has ceased to have an immediate part. In deference to this disposition we have already conceded to the greater Colonies a self-government infinitely exceeding that of any one of the

States which compose the United States, and amounting, as has been said, to a practical independence in all domestic matters. In political affairs it is almost impossible to go back; what has been given can hardly be withdrawn.

It is difficult to imagine any means by which any common revenue could be established for common Imperial purposes. A Customs Zollverein seems quite beyond the region of practical politics. One can hardly suppose such an arrangement, between countries so distant, to be practicable under any circumstances; but in our case free trade at once bars the way. We do not levy duty on any considerable product of the self-governing Colonies; they have in our ports the same freedom as the rest of the world. The duty on their nascent wine-product is very much less in proportion than that levied on our native spirits. It must be admitted that in free trade, as in other things, we must take the drawbacks with the advantages, and if it be a drawback, it is no doubt the case that, practising free trade as good in itself, we have no longer anything to offer to others in exchange for concessions on their part. We cannot, in this shape, offer any bribe to the Colonists to induce them to admit our goods on more favourable terms than at present; and at present they generally affect high protectionist tariffs. To make any mutual arrangements possible, we must not only abandon the general principles of free trade, but we must establish differential duties in favour of the Colonies. And more than that, we must put our duties on food and raw materials. No duty on foreign manufactures would benefit the Colonies, for the day is not within measurable distance when there can be any question of their exporting manufactures to England on any considerable scale. The only possible plan at which the most extreme Protectionists could point would be one under which we should tax food and raw products, making a difference in favour of the Colonies—a heavy tax on those things imported from foreign countries, a lighter one on those imported from the Colonies. If there be wild dreamers who have imagined such a thing, I am sure all sensible men, be they Liberals or Conservatives, be they Free-traders or Protectionists, see that such a taxation is impossible. We may dismiss it as out of the question. A close union with the Colonies, and a common revenue, cannot be obtained on those terms.

If there is no available source of a common revenue, any arrangement for common armaments could only be effected by a cash contribution from the different portions of the Empire. It need hardly be said that any plan of that kind would involve very delicate and difficult questions. We have removed our troops from the free Colonies (a few naval and Imperial depôts excepted), and we give them free permission to raise troops of their own. Canada has, in fact, a large popular army on the United States system, and the other Colonies have troops of their own. Suggestion has hardly been made of a combined army. Besides the question of pecuniary contributions, there would be many difficulties on the subject of recruiting and pay, and especially of distribution and the needs of the various parts of the Empire in times of common danger. If we cannot have a thorough Union like that of the United States, there seem to be many reasons for not disturbing present military arrangements rashly or hastily. Even if arrangements for a common navy could really be made, there would still be some of the same difficulties as in regard to a common army. In time of danger, who is to decide on the distribution of our navy? Would there not be risk that we might be obliged to divide it among the extremities of the Empire at a time when there might be possible danger of a blow at the heart?

There is another point of view from which a too intimate relation with the Colonies might be embarrassing.

One cannot read the concurrent statements of Mr. Froude and Baron Hubner, and observe the questions surging up between labour delegates and representatives of the Colonial Governments, without feeling that there are very grave social questions in Australasia, which may some day assume a very serious form. In all countries where the Constitution is very democratic, and yet there is a powerful plutocracy, holding its own by the methods known to plutocrats in such communities, the situation is apt to be very strained, and there is danger of a capsize, unless the vessel of the State is steadied by a very large class intermediate between the plutocrats and the labourers for hire. In America this latter function is fulfilled by the preponderating mass of small farmers, and in England by the great middle class. But in Australasia the small farmers seem to be by no means so numerous and so powerful as in America, nor the middle class so preponderating as in England. If that be so, there is much more danger. And if there were serious civil differences it would be a very hard and invidious task for us to intervene, and to make use of British soldiers and sailors for the suppression of local broils. It would be like interfering between a man and his wife. I must say, I think we shall do well to avoid any such obligation. With the comparatively close union they have in America any interference of Federal troops in civil disturbances is a very difficult matter. It would be much more so in the case of a looser union with more distant self-governing Colonies.

I would revert, then, to a great degree, to the maxim "Let well alone." Let us take care lest attempts to better matters should disturb the excellent harmony now prevailing. Let us be careful how we attempt too close a union, which might lead to quarrels and difficulties. One might well sympathise with the idea of a great confederation of all the English-speaking races—of Britain with all her children.

But it is too late to hope for that in regard to our earliest Colonies. If that were possible, it might have involved the eventual transfer of the centre of gravity from London to Washington, which we would not have liked. Those Colonies which we now protect are, as has been already said, too scattered for a very close union. By all means let us establish and maintain the most friendly links, and try to put matters on such a footing that those links shall be lasting. Let us maintain the closest alliance compatible with complete self-government; but in making any changes, let us not be carried away by too large ideas. Let us rather confine ourselves to remedying the real practical difficulties which are found to exist under the present system.

With respect to the cost of common affairs, and especially the army and navy, I do incline to think that we shall do better to bear our present burden than to seek to obtain contributions from the Colonies. We can afford a good deal, and it is better to keep ourselves free from inconvenient obligations. Rather let us follow out the present course of insisting on the duty of self-defence. The great communities across the seas have already accepted that obligation, and to that we must adhere. We shall, of course, be expected to assist them in difficulties so far as we are able to do so, and we should equally look to them to assist us when they can. But there would be no definite and binding obligation on either side. The amount and form of assistance must be regulated by circumstances, and the position and necessities of each party. The aid which we should get from the Colonies would be the friendly and voluntary aid of an allied brotherhood. Already they have shown a disposition to render such aid. I cannot but think that the Soudan expedition was not the most fortunate occasion which could have been chosen for the initiation of Colonial assistance to the Mother Country, but it was the occasion of showing much friendly sentiment.

If, then, the result of examination be that neither in regard to civil, commercial, and revenue affairs, nor in regard to a combined army and navy, can we have such a union with the free Colonies as that of the United States, there only remains to arrange the mode by which questions arising between ourselves and the Colonies may be settled, and especially questions relating to foreign Powers and the dealings with savage or comparatively uncivilised tribes and peoples beyond the Colonial limits. Indeed, distance and complete self-government render it almost impossible that any very serious questions should arise directly between ourselves and the Colonies. It is only in regard to foreign and extra-Colonial native affairs that difficulties arise.

In dealing with these limited matters, I think it must be said at the outset that we must not be too timid—not seem so nervously anxious about the so-called Empire on which the sun never sets, that we are afraid to hold our own, and are liable to be sat upon, not only in matters which concern ourselves alone, but in those which may embarrass us with foreign Powers or involve injustice to native races whom we are bound to protect. Petting is all very well up to a certain point; but there is a point beyond which it is bad for all parties. Indulgence begets the demand for more and more indulgence. The overpetted child becomes a source of trouble and unfriendliness. I will not conceal my view that, as we are situated, a friendly separation would be better than an unequal partnership on terms unfair to the Mother Country, and which might lead to bickerings and unpleasantnesses. Now that the old jealousies due to the mode of our separation from the United States have died away there seems a happy prospect that we may re establish a close intimacy with them, almost as great as if we were formally united, and such as may render war between two friendly peoples of the same kith and kin almost impossible. We emigrate or seek our fortunes in the United States just as freely as if they were still British. Facilities of communication have almost bridged the Atlantic. The interchange of ideas by means of a common literature, and the interchange of wives by more and more frequent intermarriage, are making us again one people. Only some established and recognised system of tribunals and international arbitration seems wanting to smooth over all difficulties. So, if for any reason it came to political separation, it might be in the case of Canada, and that would undoubtedly relieve us of great trans-Atlantic responsibilities. Australia is so distant that it may be that when generations grow up which are Australasian rather than British, and the Australasian Colonies have greatly increased in numbers and strength, they may desire a separation which shall not interfere with most intimate and friendly relations. If these things did happen, I think we should still have ample scope for our energies in Asia, Africa, and the islands of the tropical seas. But I say so much merely by way of insisting that the union shall be on terms fair to the Mother Country, and not on terms under which we must continually concede everything. So long as union can be continued on fair terms, I quite agree that it is desirable to continue it—that it is not for us prematurely to cut off children who wish to stay with us.

The free Colonies are already considerable countries, but we must not exaggerate their present position in regard to the Mother Country. According to the last returns, Canada and Newfoundland number a population of about 4,500,000; Australia (including Western Australia), Tasmania, and New Zealand, a little over 3,000,000; or say, in all, seven and three-quarter millions, as compared to over thirty-six millions in the Mother Country—say a little over one-fifth. A few years hence, adding in the Cape Colony, the proportion may reach one-fourth of our population. But it must be remembered that these Colonies are not increasing so rapidly as the United States, while we also, notwithstanding emigration, have still a considerable annual increase. The Cape Colony, too, can hardly be included in the comparison, as so large a part of the population are Africans.

We must consider, too, whether we are to deal with single Colonies or with groups of Colonies. The federation of Canada seems to be a great success, both as regards internal politics and as making Canada an independent, self-supporting nation. I should think the sooner Newfoundland is joined to the rest the better. In Australia, too, it seems an absurd anomaly that adjoining territories, like New South Wales and Victoria, should be walled out from one another by Customs barriers. The sooner they can settle such matters the better for them. But when it comes to the Mother Country taking an active part in suggesting and promoting federation in Africa or Australia, I cannot help thinking that such movements have been a good deal prompted by the desire to get rid of responsibilities, and to turn over to federated Colonies troublesome external relations, the control over native territories, and the conduct of native wars. That may be all very well if the object is to prepare the way for eventual Colonial independence; but if it is carried too far, it must, I think, tend in that direction. For instance, I think that a very great mistake was made when, in the scheme for a permissive Australian federation, one of the common subjects was declared to be the relations of Australasia with the islands of the Pacific, a concession which really seems to involve a separate foreign policy. I will discuss later the general question of the advisability of turning over to the Colonies the dominion over territories not free. In this place I only desire again to point out that this relation of the Australians with places beyond the seas must raise the difficult and dangerous question of a sea-going Colonial navy. A federated Australia or Australasia, managing its own relations with the islands of the Pacific, must have a navy, small or great. Naval officers in their ships are nowadays a sort of armed diplomats; and it is impossible that we should have in the same seas two British navies under different commanders and a different control. The day may come when we may withdraw ourselves altogether from the South Pacific, and leave that region entirely to the Colonists. But, except in the improbable event of all foreign European Powers consenting to withdraw also, I think that must lead to independence. We could not remain responsible for foreign relations which we did not control. Meantime, we must insist on unity of naval control on the high seas, as well as on a single diplomacy for the whole Empire.

But how to get that single diplomacy—that is the question, and a very difficult question it is to solve.

At present, the Agents of each Colony are present in London, and no doubt the Secretary of State for Foreign Affairs consults them in all matters affecting the interests of those whom they represent; but still the difficulty remains—if the Colonies are not satisfied with the results of our diplomatic action, we are put in the dilemma that we must either give in to them, or offend them; and if we give in to them, we may offend foreign Powers.

It has been suggested that to deal with such matters there should be a sort of council of the Empire, in which delegates from the Colonies should meet British representatives. But those who have made such suggestions have also pointed out the difficulties which might arise. The only case at all parallel seems to be that of Austro-Hungary. But there you have only two countries to settle matters between them, and the personal authority of the sovereign, still great, forms an important connecting link. And after all, matters go on very indifferently. As regards the external affairs of the dual Empire, there is often a great deal of friction and much dissatisfaction on one side or the other. In a general council of the British Empire the interests represented would be much more numerous and sometimes quite as conflicting. In any such council the population, importance, and weight of the Mother Country would entitle her to a preponderating representation; she could not consent to be ruled by her Colonies. Each Colony, on the other hand, might be little satisfied with the decision of a body in which its representatives would be but a very small minority. They would probably be as little as now inclined to accept as final and binding the decisions of the representatives of the Mother Country, and just as little inclined to defer to the decision of the other Colonies and possessions of the Crown; for the circumstances of these British possessions vary so greatly that one has but little in common with the other. The view of practical men seems to be that the decision by a mere majority of such a body as we have been describing would not settle our difficulties and insure general acquiescence and content.

It is evident, too, that such a body would be much too large directly to conduct diplomatic negotiations. That function must necessarily be delegated; and how to obtain a delegation whose action would be accepted by all? What is to be done then? Can we go on as now and trust to the chapter of accidents and expedients of the moment to settle each case as it arises? I think not; we cannot be always running the risk of friction and bad understandings. Something must be settled.

What we want is by some means or other to relieve ourselves of the odium and risk of deciding for the Colonies on our own responsibility, and to get over the difficulty of enforcing our decisions. The solution to which I incline is the establishment of some sort of standing tribunal of reference and arbitration of so judicial a character that all must bow to its decisions. If we could obtain such a body whose authority should be recognised by all the subjects of the Crown, its decisions might well be final and binding in all questions which might arise directly between ourselves and the Colonists. And as regards questions with foreign Powers, the same tribunal might decide as between us and the Colonies what it is right to give or accept in the general interest. If such a system were established on our side we might hope that foreign Powers might on their part meet us in a similar spirit, and that the result might be some recognised system of national arbitration which would do much to promote the peace of the world. Already in America proposals for a tribunal of international arbitration have been made and have found much favour. It would be a very great blessing if we could have a tribunal of that character, to whom could be referred at once, without more ado, fishery and other disputes.

It is, it seems to me, certain that if we are to have a united Empire we must have some means of dealing as one Empire with external affairs and obtaining decisions binding on all. Perhaps something may come of the official references which have now been made. The subject is far too difficult to dogmatise; by all means let us have all the advice and assistance which we can get towards settling it, whether at home or from the Colonies.

Since the above was written the circular of the Colonial Office to the Colonies has been published, and proves to be as cautious as I could possibly desire—in fact, even more cautious than I have been, for, confining the discussion to defence and communication, it distinctly bars the question of Colonial Federation, and does not touch that of a common diplomacy. So far as it goes it seems quite on the lines which I have suggested, and I cannot but approve of it.

It must be said, however, that a large proportion of the cases in which we have difficulty in maintaining Imperial authority, fulfilling our obligations, and at the same time satisfying the more adventurous of the Colonists, are those dealings with indigenous tribes, to which the term "foreign affairs," in the dignified sense, is hardly applied; and I have already said that I propose to reserve that subject for separate examination.

There is, however, one matter, involving questions of internal self-government of the Colonies, of which something must here be said. Both Australia and Western Canada are so situated that much of the Chinese outflow tends in those directions. If things were allowed to take their course, it seems very likely that the Chinese populations might dispute the occupation of those countries with the white race. Without going into motives, it is enough to say that the whites object to share the country with the Chinamen; and if the Colonies are wholly self-governing, one can hardly say that they are not entitled to decide for themselves that Australasia and Columbia shall be regions of whites rather than of mixed populations. At any rate, the Royal Assent has not been refused to Australian laws of a highly restrictive character directed against the Chinese. We cannot go back from that. It seems hardly consistent with our treaties, and the liberty which we claim for British subjects in China; but I suppose we must just tell the Chinese that we can no more answer for the Colonies in the way of free trade in emigration, than we can in the way of commercial free trade.

But beyond this, it happens that parts of Australia, its northern coasts, are really tropical in climate; the low-lying regions there are not well suited for white labour; the enterprisers there, sugar-planters, etc., are anxious enough to get coloured labour. They do not seem to be satisfied with free Chinese immigration, for the Chinese are too independent, troublesome, and expensive; they have set themselves to obtain coloured labour of another kind, procured not by mere voluntary free immigration, but imported under what is called the "indenture" system, which means compulsory service for a term of years. So long as this labour is strictly confined to the lower class of work in the completely tropical low-lying regions of the north, the free populations have not wholly objected; but they have insisted that it shall not go beyond this. The consequence is, that these coloured labourers are not only bound to labour for the term of their indentures, but cannot at any time gain a footing as completely free men. They are forbidden certain parts of the country, and certain callings. This rule applies to labourers imported under indenture from India or Ceylon, as well as to the South Sea islanders called Kanakas. I will not here enter upon the abuses of the labour importation from the islands; but on general grounds I have always strongly objected, and do object, to any emigration fostered and aided or protected by our Government, if the emigrants are not (when, at least, their indentures are completed), to be entirely free, and entitled to all the privileges of free men. The Indian Government has always insisted on security for good and fair treatment before they facilitated the emigration of indentured labourers from India; and in Crown Colonies the Crown is supposed to have the means of insuring the fulfilment of these obligations. But in self-governing Colonies it is not so. I doubt whether it is good for white Colonies that there should be a part of their territory in the position of the Southern States of the American Union. If the main portion of Australia is to be a white man's country, it will probably be better that it should all be so, and that the best should be made that under the circumstances can be made of the smaller portion that is tropical. But, at any rate, I think we should have neither art nor part in the introduction of a population that is to remain in any degree in a servile and inferior position. If the Australians will have coloured people at all, they must be fully and entirely free.

Nor do I think that it would answer to make Northern Queensland a Crown Colony, to be permanently ruled by British officials in the interest of a varied population. We have difficulty enough in managing such Colonies in the best of circumstances; but to attempt to do so in close contact with free Colonies, and with no natural boundary between, would be pretty sure to eventuate in great difficulties. The North Queensland planters, anxious to get coloured labour, might accept Crown Government for a time, but they would be pretty sure to put forward claims for local management sooner or later.

There is another immigration question. According to Baron Hubner and others, the Americans are beginning to welcome even European immigration less than they did, and there would seem to be at present something of that feeling in Australia. I do not know that it has yet gone beyond protest against State-aided immigration. But both in America and Australia there seems to be jealousy of receiving not only those tainted with crime but even those tainted with poverty. The Colonies are rather too anxious to get only the cream of our labouring people, and to leave all the residuum to us. It is the natural tendency of things that many of the most vigorous emigrate from our shores and leave the less vigorous behind. Already that process has, I take it, materially affected our social position and the great question of the poor. It would be hard that this tendency should be strengthened by arbitrary interference with the free circulation of the population, good or indifferent, throughout the British Empire. So long as the Colonies assist emigration they are, of course, free to choose whom they will assist, but if they cease to assist they should not restrict the flow. Yet, if they did some day do so—if they too closely examined into the condition and means of British subjects approaching their shores, or even subjected them to arbitrary rules and restrictions, somewhat of the nature of those which they apply to the Chinese, could we submit to that? It is to be hoped that they will not try us in that way.

On the other hand, we must be careful how we get into trouble with them by promoting emigration in a way which might bring about differences. I do not here enter at large on the subject of what is called State-directed Colonisation; for the question whether it is desirable to get rid of a portion of our population is rather a home question of social politics. But one word may be said on the matter as affecting our relations with the Colonies. If we had a surplus population of small farmers and agricultural labourers, and if we had retained the control over Colonial lands and some control over Colonial administration, something might have been done by us to promote colonisation. But, apart from the disputable case of the Scotch crofters of the Western Islands, and the Irish of the portion of Ireland yet overpopulated, we have not too many of the farming and gardening classes: they are already almost too much drawn into our towns; and, if we had them, the distribution of Colonial lands lies with the Colonies. The principal demand for State-aided emigration is not on the part of farmers or even agricultural labourers, but rather on that of the non-agricultural classes in times of depression and distress.

It is an evil of our system of capitalist and labourer for hire that there must be great variations in the demand for labour. Whether our population is really in excess of our requirements, or whether, in the event of a revival of trade, all surplus hands might be again wanted, is a question which I do not pretend to answer. But, at any rate, if the State is to promote emigration from this country, it can for the most part only be in the shape of assisting our people to emigrate, and leaving the Colonies or countries to which they go to deal with them when they come. In any attempt to make any bargain with the Colonies on the subject they have been far too exacting. And then we always come to the difficulty that if we send the poverty-stricken, they may be rejected; if we send our best hands only, that is hardly fair to ourselves. On the whole it seems safest as long as possible to trust to the improvement of facilities for the circulation of our people throughout the world and to free-trade in population.

CHAPTER III.

POSSESSIONS, AND SETTLEMENTS NOT SELF-GOVERNING.

LEAVING now the free self-governing Colonies of the temperate zones, we come to the vast British possessions of another character—those in warmer climes, generally inhabited by numerous coloured races, and in which the European is not so much a Colonist in the proper sense, as an administrator, an enterpriser, a director, and employer of labour. These form a larger subject of inquiry from an administrative point of view, as we are more directly responsible for them. The white colonisation of temperate and almost unoccupied regions is, as it were, automatic, and the management of such settlements is almost from the nature of things autonomous.

Our anxieties in regard to settlements in temperate regions are also limited by the fact that there are no more temperate worlds to conquer—we have got them all. The globe is limited, and if we look around we shall find no more. Parts of South America are not fully occupied, but others have forestalled us there, and southern Europeans are to some degree filling up the void. We shall hardly attempt new dominions there.

On the other hand, where we come into contact with considerable native races, organised settlement and dominion can hardly go on automatically; it must be protected, regulated, and restricted from dangerous excesses. The Indian Empire could never have been acquired and consolidated as a British possession by mere uncontrolled adventurers. Moreover, the limit of new fields for extension of dominions of this character has not been reached. In Asia, Africa, and Oceania we are still advancing, and very large questions are raised by actual or possible extensions.

Before going further, I wish to say something of the fitness of our countrymen for rule and enterprise in dominions of this latter class. I have suggested that, as proper agricultural Colonists, our modern ways have made us less apt and less ready to plod steadily to success than some other peoples among whom small farming is still a normal occupation. But, this exception made, the people of the United Kingdom are really unrivalled for adventure, enterprise, and the development of the world. As a Scotchman, I need not speak vainly, for the testimony is universal that the Scotch are pre-eminent in these qualities. But let us speak of the United Kingdom as a whole. There is not only the great middle class always ready to send missionaries of progress all over the world, but upwards, to the very highest class, the same thing is the case. Primogeniture may have something to do with it. But be that as it may, it is certain that we have an enormous and ever-increasing class of young men (extending downwards, too, as education extends) who are somewhat above the class of mere manual labourers, and are full of the courage, the enterprise, and the endurance which leads them to seek their fortunes all over the world. I say somewhat above the mere manual labour class with every regard for the dignity of labour, which I hope is coming to be more and more acknowledged, and which our young men very often realise in practice when they go abroad; but I only mean that they are qualified to direct and stimulate the labour of others; and in this respect I think they are, on the whole, superior to any other people. The Germans may be, in fact are, in some respects, better educated, more patient, more thrifty and frugal, and less rash than the Britisher; but for pluck and go, and the qualities of a ruler and adventurer, I think that those of us who have seen our countrymen struggling against difficulties in all sorts of circumstances and all parts of the world, must admit that they are probably the best of all. I don't compare with Americans, for they are our own blood, and have occupation enough in their own territories; but, compared to all others—French, or German, or Dutch, or be they who they may—I do not think any people could have done all we have done. Perhaps the Germans are, in some respects, better traders. They make way and thrive sometimes when we do not think the profit sufficient; but Baron Hubner admits that they are scarcely so enterprising. The Dutch have done great things in their way, but they no longer advance. With all their dash and freedom from religious and other prejudices, the French of these days do not seem at all successful, either as Colonisers or administrators of new countries. The Russians are only beginning to try their hand. I do not think that any other country could have done in India what we have done.

As Colonisers and enterprisers we have only one fault—that too great haste to be rich by short cuts, which I have mentioned as resulting from the circumstances of the present day. But we may hope that, as times become quieter and competition leads to more modest expectations, the evils resulting from this too ambitious spirit will be abated.

There is, however, always this special difficulty, that in addition to the legitimate fortune-seekers, the out-of-the-way seas and islands of the world swarm with an inferior class of adventurers—the scum and offscourings of society—men for whom the old countries have become too hot, or sailors who find the discipline of their own profession too much for them, and who have dropped off into very rough adventure wherever they may have chanced to be cast. A very large proportion of these men are English-speakers, and presumably most of them are British subjects. But when they are in trouble with British authorities they are apt to call themselves Americans, and it is difficult to identify them. The police of the far-off seas is a very difficult and complicated matter.

In regard to adventurers, good and bad alike, it is too apt to happen that, if they are not sufficiently controlled, they drag us into situations and obligations from which it is difficult to escape, without our having any choice in the matter. If we are to extend our Empire, it ought to be done with our consent, and not at the will of individuals who go into strange places at their own risk and then call on the British power to follow them. But in practice it is very difficult to adjust these things.

However, all difficulties notwithstanding, the existence among us of a great and ever-increasing class of young men more or less educated, who are ready to seek employment and fortune beyond the narrow limits of our own islands, is a reason and justification for foreign extensions where they can be legitimately made, and provided we do not carry them to that point of imprudence that, in scattering our power and resources, we may too much weaken the heart and centre. None of us can fail to be aware of the vast supply of this youth growing up around us, and which it is very desirable to utilise to the best advantage. So far I quite feel that there is a great deal to be said for foreign extensions. But then, before we go on piling up territory upon territory, we must make sure that we have made the most and the best of the vast territories which we already have. And we must weigh the risk of weakening the centre, which I have just mentioned.

Let us see how we stand. We are a people of some thirty-six millions, and an increasing people—but that increase is considerably diminished by emigration. We have immense manufactures and commerce, and an unprecedented accumulation of wealth; but others have learned to compete with us in our trades, and we do not advance so fast as we did. Our vast wealth—or at any rate, the home and the centre of it—is in these British Islands, where it is gathered and stored in enormous piles. We have been enabled to do this in safety, owing to the immunity which our insular position and strong navy have given us. But we have never had a strong army in point of numbers; our people have not submitted to that system of conscription which fills Continental armies, and industrial hive that we are, it is scarcely possible that we should submit to conscription for foreign service; no foreign Powers have attempted that on a large scale. Our army, then, is a voluntary army, and a very expensive army. There is a limit to the number of recruits who are forthcoming. Under such a system, if we do pretty well for our present force in times of trade depression like the present, we might have great difficulty if trade again became prosperous. Great as our resources are, our revenue is not increasing as it used to increase, and we have to spend so much on the navy as the first necessity of our existence, that we cannot afford to be regardless of expense with respect to the army. Already our army is by far the hardest worked army in the world; under the most peace-proclaiming of Governments it has been recently engaged in endless wars; and at this moment the exhausting drains upon it in Burmah, Egypt and elsewhere make it very difficult to keep our regiments efficient. The normal garrison of India must always be a very great strain on our personal resources. For years past the mass of our battalions at home have been in a state which has caused much concern. After supplying the demand of the battalions abroad they are like spent fish, emaciated and exhausted; or at best their ranks are filled with immature and untaught boy recruits. In days when such gigantic armaments exist in Europe, and when the new and untried character of naval armaments renders the naval warfare of the future very experimental and uncertain, there are many who think that our great and tempting wealth is hardly sufficiently protected at home. While there is a very great drain of our army to India and the Colonies, we have not yet succeeded in availing ourselves of the services of Indian or other soldiers beyond their own countries to any very large extent, except on very special occasions.

On these grounds it is that a large school of politicians think that there is danger in too great and too rapid an extension of the Empire. Of this doctrine Mr. Gladstone was the exponent and the apostle. Yet it is a strange irony of fate—and shows how much, in the absence of any clearly settled policy, we are dragged on, whether we like it or no —that since he so formally and forcibly expounded this doctrine in 1880, the Empire has expanded more rapidly than at almost any former period. Events may have led up to the annexation of Burmah and the arrangement by which we guaranteed the territories of Abdur Rahman, and so accepted a military responsibility beyond the frontiers of India extending to the Oxus and the Hareerood. But also we have occupied Egypt, and engaged in several campaigns in Egypt and the Soudan. We have made very large annexations in South Africa, in West Africa, in Borneo, in New Guinea, to say nothing of Port Hamilton and other smaller things. It is time to take stock of our actual and possible liabilities; perhaps when we go into particulars we may find that we have already gone so far that it is only in certain directions there is room to go much farther. One might be the more inclined to justify all that has been done, if one could suppose that there was a design of reaching limits where we might rest; but I am afraid that, even if other things could lead one to the view that there was any method in our policy, several of the recent annexations would not square with the theory just mentioned—especially in Africa.

CHAPTER IV.

INDIA.

INDIA is far too large a subject to discuss here in full, but we must look at it in a few aspects which affect the Imperial question. There can be no doubt that within the whole country, or countries, comprised in what may be called the natural limits of India—from the Indus to the eastern hills, and from the Himalayas to the ocean—the people have so long been accustomed to despotic and foreign dominion, that they are, or were, without that national pride and impatience which lead so many peoples to resist alien rule. Throughout the whole of India proper they have accepted our rule without any popular struggle. From the time we overcame or supplanted the former rulers, and obtained military domination, the people have easily submitted. If ever there were a government in India sprung from the people, it was that of the Sikhs in the Punjab; and of all the peoples of India the Punjabees were the most manly, self-governing, and independent. Yet, under the influence of a very judicious and successful administration, they accepted our rule, after victory, without any popular resistance whatever, and soon became our best friends and allies.

One thing only is necessary to the contentment of the people of India under our rule, and that is, that we should not interfere too much. The fact is that a sort of patriotism and a spirit of independence are not wanting to them, but are rather local and tribal than national. In one sense they were, as we found them, the most self-governing people in the world—that is to say, they had a faculty of managing their own affairs in their own villages and caste and trade guilds, quite independent of the government of the day, and could carry on wonderfully when there was no government at all. That is what was done by the village communities which survived the crash of Empire, and kept society together in the hundred years of anarchy which preceded the establishment of our rule. Hence it is that our Government is most satisfactory to the people in its early stages, before we have learned to interfere too much. I believe that our early rule in the Punjab was a model in this respect; and though we have not always followed the same lines, I think it is not to be denied that so far our rule in India, as a whole, has been good both for the governing and the governed.

But the future is not so clear. The English (and in this I speak of English as distinguished from Scotch and Irish) owe so much of their own freedom to law and lawyers, that they have come to have an almost superstitious veneration for those institutions. They hardly sufficiently distinguish between law and justice, and think any people must be happy among whom they have established laws, courts, and many lawyers, after the pattern to which they are accustomed. These courts are very intolerant of laws and institutions other than their own. And it has long been the complaint in most Provinces of India that the old self-acting institutions have been sapped and destroyed, and that there has arisen a reign of lawyers, worse, some say, than that of the Pindarrees. That is an old complaint, but one which has not been remedied. And now quite another difficulty has sprung up. English education has so much spread among a generation which has forgotten the ills from which we rescued their fathers, that there has sprung up a class who, on political and personal grounds, dispute and resent our assumed superiority, and use the excessive freedom of the Press, of Speech, and of Lawyerdom which we have given, to decry us and dispute with us. The future is not so smooth and easy as the past has been.

Then as regards our military position. It must be realised that the events of the Mutiny not only led to a great increase of the European force which we are obliged to supply from England, but also to a great decrease of the army of India as a whole. As neither in men nor in cost could we afford a European force beyond a certain limit, and as we no longer thought it safe to maintain a native army too much out of proportion to the European force, on political as well as on financial grounds the army has been reduced till it is really very small indeed, when compared with the country and populations to be controlled. I have sometimes called it in that view the smallest army in the world. Of the native army which we have, only a part is robust enough to be efficient as against European forces. The total force in India consisted of about 63,000 Europeans and 126,000 natives, to which number some additions are now being made—say 200,000 all told, effectives and non-effectives together. That is the force with which we are bound to maintain order among upwards of two hundred and fifty million people (two hundred millions being our subjects and fifty millions those of Native States), and to defend them from external aggression.

Small as our Indian army is, it is, however, probably more than sufficient to keep order in our territories under present conditions, and so long as there is no panic outbreak of the population, such as affected the Sepoys in the Mutiny. But before we come to those external questions which now affect the military position of India, we must look at another question — the armament of the native princes, who rule over fifty millions of the population.

With so small an army of our own, that cannot be overlooked; we need not exaggerate in an alarmist way, but also we must not blink the situation. It is very true that up to the present most of the troops of Native States, if numerous, are in other respects somewhat contemptible. But some are efficient, and others may become so; there is no rule in the matter. It is not a mere question of the fidelity of the reigning princes themselves. They have much to lose, and are generally safe enough. But while armed forces exist, there is no saying in what direction their arms may be turned. In times of serious trouble, fires may spread to Native States. There are generally discontented elements and rival claims, and there is the uncertain spirit of mercenary troops, perhaps under very indifferent discipline. We might have princes in our camps, and their troops against us—as has happened before. Scindiah held by us in the Mutiny, but it was the Gwalior force which at the last broke away and defeated General Wyndham at Cawnpore. I think it is necessary that, holding the Indian Empire, we should effectively control both the numbers and the character of the armament of the troops of the Native States, and so arrange matters that, while useful as auxiliaries where they are wanted, they should not be dangerous. One condition to fulfil the latter object is, I think, that they should not be too closely assimilated to our troops. It was the "Contingents," the British-drilled forces in the service of the princes, rather than the purely native forces, which gave us trouble in the Mutiny; and that lesson has already been acted on.

The feudatory position of all the Native States, great and small, is now recognised, and none of them can act quite independently. Nepal must be excepted; subject to certain obligations, that is really still independent territory, and we have no control whatever over Nepalese armaments, excepting only that command over the import of arms from abroad which our geographical position may give us. As a matter of fact, the Nepalese (shrewd and civilised people that they are) have, I believe, established efficient arms factories of the modern type of their own. But their population is not very large, nor is their revenue, even with the considerable territory in the plains beneath their hills, which they owe to us. Their army, though efficient, is not large. They are deficient in cavalry, and said to have something of our own Highlanders' dread of cavalry. Down in the plains they probably could not bring into the field a force which would be very formidable to us, even if they were not friendly and prudent and alive to their own position.

Over all the other States we can exercise a large control. But still that control is generally ill-defined, and till very recently there were cases in which it was not accepted in a spirit of entire submission. Scindiah had strong military tastes, considerable military knowledge, and a not very amiable temper. He notoriously chafed under the restraints which we had imposed on him, and after long effort he had just succeeded in obtaining a far greater degree of independence than he had ever had before. The British subsidiary force which was substituted after the Mutiny for the British-officered contingent having been withdrawn, and the Gwalior Fort surrendered, he became completely master in his own territory, subject only to treaty engagements. Sir Salar Jung, again, the virtual ruler of the great State of Hyderabad, was not on the best terms with the Government of India. He fought us, it is true, with modern weapons—European agencies and the press, and political and social demonstrations in London; but still the position which he assumed made it much more difficult to control in our interests the large and miscellaneous armed forces of various kinds existing in the Hyderabad territory, and in regard to which we had no very well-defined treaty rights. But in regard to the question we are now discussing, it may almost be said (if one could use the expression) that fortune has favoured the British Government. Salar Jung, and Scindiah, and Holkar, the heads of all the most important and troublesome States, are gone. Minors and Ministers dependent on the British Government occupy a position which makes this task infinitely more easy. Lord Dufferin has just formally exercised the prerogative of installing a young Nizam at Hyderabad, and appointing a young Minister. Scindiah's territories have come under a long minority and a British-appointed Regency. The position of Holkar's family renders it little probable that his successor will affect the independent bearing of his father. The Maharajah of Cashmere is not what old Gholab Sing was, and circumstances seem to have overcome the somewhat exclusive spirit which once prevailed in that State, and have brought it much more under the control of a permanent British Resident. The chiefs of Rajpootana, never very independent, have lately, on some occasions, owed to us security against rebellious feudatories.

I think, if we are wise, we shall take advantage of favouring circumstances to put military arrangements on a permanent and satisfactory footing, and not allow things to drift on till fresh difficulties and embarrassments crop up.

Now, coming to questions of external responsibilities and defence, we naturally begin with Affghanistan. The word Affghanistan is exceedingly misleading, and its use is apt to lead to misconception. The people do not call themselves Affghans, but "Pathans." "Affghan" seems to be a term applied to them by the Persians. However, let that pass. I will use the term Affghan, as we are accustomed to it. The Affghanistan of the Affghan people is very different from Affghanistan in the sense of the dominions of the Ameer of Cabul. The ethnological boundary is the Indus. Rivers are said to be seldom true boundaries; but the upper Indus runs through a peculiar country, and there it really is the boundary between the Indian and Affghan peoples from the point where it issues from the higher mountains of the Himalaya downwards. The people beyond the river are pure Affghans all the way southwards till we come to the Belooch tribes. Within those limits, the country from the Indus to Cabul Ghuznee and Candahar is the country of the Affghan people. The Hindoo Khoosh is not included; it is inhabited by a different race. The hills north and west of Cabul and Ghuznee are held by non-Affghan peoples, and it is the same when we go beyond Candahar to the Herat country and the hills north of Herat. Still less are the tracts north of the mountains, now called Affghan Turkestan, in any degree Affghan in population.

Of the true Affghanistan, a very large proportion is not subject to the Ameer at all. We have possessed ourselves of Peshawur and the other Affghan valleys between the hills and the Indus; and beyond that the tribes are recognised to be wholly independent. The Ameer there only rules over a few valleys in which he is able to maintain a dominion. It is only among the western tribes, which seem to have some intermixture of Persian blood and character, that his rule was generally recognised; and there it is that rebellion has lately broken out. On the other hand, his suzerainty, or sovereignty, which we have lately guaranteed, extends over all the non-Affghan territories reaching to the Oxus and the Hareerood.

We are so much accustomed to look at things from our point of view only, that I think we hardly realise the feelings of the Affghan rulers in regard to our occupation of the Affghan valleys on the side of the Indus. The throne of Cabul is at best a bed of thorns; the only chance the ruler has is by making the most of the more open valleys, and drawing from thence the resources with which he may bribe or control the hillmen. From this point of view the Affghan territories we hold are an enormous cantle cut out of his dominions. The Peshawur valley alone is something much more considerable than is generally recognised. The population of that district was, according to the last census, close on 600,000, occupying a fertile territory, much of it almost a garden. The Kohat and Bannoo valleys number another half-million. Altogether there must be quite a million and a half Affghans in the trans-Indus districts of the Punjab.

When we compare this territory and population with the scanty total over which the Ameer exercises a really effective control, we may well understand the feelings of Dost Mahommed and his successors in regard to its alienation. It is true that it was not we who conquered it, but Runjeet Singh. Runjeet, however, had held it but a short time, and had scarcely brought it into real subjection. He did little more than hold it as a sort of pledge, entrusting the civil administration to a branch of the Affghan ruling family, and the military garrison to the well-known European General, Avitabile, who kept the people down rather by continual martial severities than by real conquest.

I have always thought that it would have been very well for all parties if, when we annexed the Punjab, we had given back the Affghan valleys to the Ameer, with or without conditions. We should have rid ourselves of a most troublesome and unpaying task; we should have earned such gratitude and contentment of the Ameer as an Affghan is capable of; and, what is more important, we should have been able to make him in some sort responsible for the protection of our frontier from the incursions of hill tribes, and we should have had something quite under our thumb to come down upon in case in any matter he caused us dissatisfaction, instead of the present situation, in which we cannot touch him without a great expedition to Cabul and Candahar. Possessed, too, of the valleys we now hold, he would have had those resources, in the absence of which we are obliged to give him a large annual subsidy to enable him barely to hold his own. Practically we have all the expense and all the odium of our occupation of the trans-Indus territory, and pay over the gross revenue to the Ameer. And the situation now is this, that while the Affghan valleys on the side of India are definitively held by us, and the Ameer has nothing to hope for there, on the other side he holds Herat and Affghan Turkestan, but holds these territories at the mercy of the neighbouring Russians, save only that right of assistance from us which he has acquired if he chooses to call us in, but of which he seems discreetly inclined to say "Timeo Danaos."

We have not only incurred responsibilities involving serious risks in Affghanistan, but we have already, in the Penjdeh affair, felt the bitterness of the situation. We are a strange people; we cry out and make a terrible fuss about dangers and difficulties which are very far off, and possible remote advantages gained by foreign Powers in remote regions, and yet when we get a real slap in the face, under circumstances that make it difficult to deal with, we sometimes take it very quietly and quite overlook it. I doubt if, short of a very great disaster, anything more humiliating to us than that Penjdeh affair ever occurred. I am certainly no Russophobe, but I must say that I thought the conduct of the Russians on that occasion brutal in the extreme. It was not merely a question of the Affghans extending their flank half a mile when it came to a fight; in time of peaceable negotiations by two important European Commissions, and after a formal promise that the Russians should not advance, the Russian general deliberately advanced several marches, and came right on the Affghan position. The Affghans had nothing for it but to fight, or let the Russians brush past to their rear, if even that they might have done without actual immediate attack. If ever a fight was provoked the Russians provoked that fight. The Affghans had British political officers in their camp, and acted entirely on the advice of these officers, the actual conduct of the fight apart. When the Affghans were crushed and massacred, these officers had to fly to the headquarters of the British Commission. And when, to avoid risk of collision with a Power with whom we were not at war, the British Commissioner himself, with his whole camp, had to retreat and cross the mountains, the elements seemed to fight against us. That terrible storm in which our people were caught completed our discomfiture. Probably our mission sent to settle a boundary dispute went out on too large a scale, and with too much pomp and circumstance. The Indian press and Indian opinion forced that on the Government. But when the bedraggled and miserable wreck of that grand Commission, hastily retreating before the Russians, reached the Persian frontiers after that dreadful snow-storm, our worst enemies could not have wished us a more sorry fate; and the Russians could not have had a more complete humiliation of the British, and exaltation of themselves, in the eyes of the tribes of those parts—which was probably the object they aimed at, rather than the possession of a trumpery village, which the result proved that they might probably have got by negotiation.

I am one of the very least likely to be carried away by warlike excitement, but I never felt so stirred in that direction as when Mr. Gladstone made his famous oration on Penjdeh; an occasion in which he seemed to me to rise to a greater height of stirring eloquence than on any other occasion on which I have heard him. We were afterwards inclined to think that his spirit-stirring defiance led to the acceptance of an arbitration, which would have been a great triumph for the advocates of a peaceable settlement of disputes. Why the arbitration came to naught is a mystery which, perhaps, we shall never know; but as two successive Governments agreed in letting it drop and refusing all explanation, we must presume that there were good reasons for that course. Humiliated as we were, we were saved from the dire necessity of war by the very practical and unimpulsive view taken by Abdur Rahman, the Ameer of Cabul. We were bound to assist him in repelling unprovoked aggression; and in the view of Mr. Gladstone and of most of us this was an aggression most unprovoked. But the Ameer knew the Russians, knew us, and knew his own territory; he knew how little valuable to him was the sovereignty over a few Turkomans, who were rather of the nature of wolves that he had got by the ears than good subjects. He knew how much of his territory was at the mercy of the Russians if he quarrelled with them, and he did not know how far we should be successful in repelling them, or how far his subjects would tolerate us as his allies. So he very quietly said, "Losses *will* happen": he put up with the loss of his troops, surrendered the disputed villages, did not invite us to repel the Russians, and so the matter ended. Anything is better than war, and we are very well out of it. But we must not treat the matter lightly, and forget it; we must take the lesson to heart. Such events may occur again, and we may not so fortunately get out of the obligation of fighting a great European Power in Central Asia, far away from our own frontier and means of communication, and near the points where the Russians have established their garrisons and communications. It is very dangerous and difficult ground, and we must be very wary and careful in our dealings.

Baron Hubner is very good on the subject of Herat, the so-called "key of India." As he says, in that case we are very unfortunate, "for the key is hanging at the enemy's gate." Herat is no more the key than many other places; but no doubt the approach of Russia so far, her setting her foot on the hills near Herat, *does* mark a stage on her onward progress. The mistake on our part would be, as the Baron says, to "put four hundred miles of desert between themselves and their base of operations by going to meet their opponent." Yet that is just what we have pledged ourselves to do in certain eventualities.

For the present our best security seems to be in the prudent and wary character of the Ameer, and the reasonable expectation that he will keep to the line of policy which he has already adopted in very trying circumstances. They are a robust people, these Affghans, and equal to the best in diplomacy and the rest of it, in spite of all that has been said against them and their undoubted faults. Not only was Dost Mahommed a very remarkable man, practical beyond the wont of Orientals, but his descendants seem to be much stronger men than we are accustomed to find in the families of great men, Oriental or other. Sher Allee after all seems to have been a man of much character, and Abdur Rahman really seems, take him all in all, to have been a great success. The new kingdom of Cabul has lasted much longer than, I confess, I ever thought it would. But Abdur Rahman cannot last for ever—we hear of gout and rebellion—there is no saying how long he will last. We may not be so fortunate next time; it will be difficult to find another of his great and hard experience. The Affghans are a wilful people, and we may not—I would like to say shall not—be in the position to nominate an Ameer as the price of our own withdrawal, as was the case when we handed over the country to Abdur Rahman and went away. Of all things we must beware of dynastic pledges. If we get into anything of that kind we shall be involved in that legality our craze for which is so embarrassing in dealing with Orientals: we shall be bound to support the legitimate heir rather than the strongest, most competent and most successful man, according to the fashion of Orientals and the doctrine well set forth by Lord Lawrence in dealing with Cabul affairs. In my opinion we must treat our obligations as strictly personal to the present Ameer, and not pledge ourselves one step beyond.

For the rest I think we must still trust a good deal to that which in the past we might have relied on to save us much anxiety and expenditure, namely, that the Russians have their difficulties as well as ourselves; that near as they now are to the Ameer's dominions, it will cost them a great deal of money yet to make effective, for large forces and a great commissariat, the overland communications with distant Russia; that their finances are not flourishing, but very much the contrary; that their Central Asian territories are neither productive nor paying; and that, after all, the Russians have objects nearer their hearts and nearer home than India; that probably they have not so much coveted India as desired to establish a raw place where they could make us wince, and to accelerate the lesson we seem to be now learning, that Constantinople is not so very much a British interest after all.

Still, when all is said, there is no denying that the bugbear which has frightened us so much for fifty years, when it was but a bugbear, has now become so far a reality that the outposts of a great European Power are really within measurable distance of our Indian outposts; that we can no longer consider India to be a country divided from the whole world, and that our military and defensive arrangements must be modified accordingly.

Probably we are right in spending a good deal of money in completing our communications along the frontier. We can, I suppose, hardly go back from the location we have made in the high country about Quettah. And if we can find a spot there more healthy than the present Quettah Cantonment appears to be, it may be a not unfavourable position for European troops overlooking the Indus valley as well as guarding the frontier. For the rest in the matter of fortifications our military authorities will no doubt consider not only the advantage of great fortifications in certain eventualities, but also the inconvenience of locking up much of our small army in garrisoning them at all times. At best this frontier question must be a source of very considerable anxiety to us, military and financial.

On the other side of India we have a very great territory on our hands in Burmah, and it must be thoroughly realised that Burmah is a country entirely outside of and different from India, not only geographically but ethnologically. The people there are totally different from the Indians in race, religion, character, habits, and political feelings, and our experience of India is no sort of guide in Burmah. Burmah requires, too, a military garrison, which can in no sense be considered a mere advance division of the Indian army protecting India just as much as if stationed farther back, which is very much the position of the force in the Punjab. For practical purposes there has hitherto been no connection between India and Burmah by land; it is a possession with which we only communicate by sea. The holding of Burmah makes us no whit more secure in India. That possession, therefore, must be judged on its own merits.

In early days, while I was an advocate for the extension of our Indian Empire to its natural frontier on the Indus, I opposed not only the extension beyond the Indus, but also the acquisition of Lower Burmah. That country has turned out to be, under our rule, an immense granary for the supply of rice to the world; and while not admitting the claim of the people at Rangoon that Lower Burmah supplies a great surplus to the Indian Empire (because that calculation omits a fair share of the common Imperial expenses), I have freely confessed in Parliament and elsewhere that it pays well, and has turned out a productive and profitable possession. But there was always the difficulty that our province of Lower Burmah had no natural frontier, and the risk that, as has generally happened in such cases, we should be dragged farther on by the force of circumstances sooner or later. That is just what has now happened.

There are those who assume that because Lower Burmah pays there is every ground for confidence that Upper Burmah will pay also. But that confidence is manifestly based on a totally false foundation, for Lower Burmah pays solely and entirely by rice, whereas Upper Burmah, so far from producing rice largely, imports it largely. Whatever the productions and the merits of Upper Burmah may prove to be, they are not those of Lower Burmah.

Then Lower Burmah has a large element of Peguan population (or at least blood), different from the pure Burmans, and more accustomed to subjection. We are consoled for the popular resistance now going on in Upper Burmah by being told that the same thing happened in Lower Burmah, but that it quieted down at last. Those who take a less sanguine view, point out that while Upper Burmah was independent there was room for an exchange of populations. The Burmans who were discontented with our rule went to Upper Burmah, while others, who did not like the Burmese government, came down to our territories. And they observe that, after all, in the recent troubles we have had some of our worst disquietudes in the lower province, even very far away from the old frontier.

Certain it is that the best and most reliable officers of experience in the country have long resisted an advance. But the Burmese were not so cautious as the Affghans and the Nepalese. While resisting British domination they did not exclude foreigners from their country—they seem rather to have desired to utilise them, and make money by them. The British merchants of Bombay and Rangoon got their fingers in, and were very anxious to introduce the whole hand. The cry of the local mercantile community has long been for an advance, and British Chambers of

Commerce have sympathised with them and backed them up in a very active way.

Our diplomacy, too, has not been fortunate. We could not agree with the Burmese Monarch on the great Shoe question, and some other matters, and in European fashion we showed our displeasure by withdrawing our Agent. The Burmese King, however, taking a practical view, looked on the departure of the British Agent as a happy riddance, leaving him free to do as he liked; and he took considerable advantage of his liberty. We did not see it in the same light. When bickerings arose, the King ostentatiously sought the alliance of European Powers, and allowed French and other adventurers to talk very big. There is no doubt that it was what I have sometimes called the "French scare," which overcame the scruples of our officers, and enabled the annexationists to have their way. Burmah so much differs from India that I have not pretended to any decided opinion in the matter. I had very great confidence in that model officer, Sir Charles Bernard, and was ready to admit (in the then absence of official information) that if he thought an advance necessary, he was probably right.

When the first Blue Book appeared, I must say my impression was that if we had no stronger case for annexation than that, it was hardly a sufficiently strong case. It was one which rested principally on mercantile grievances. The French Government had withdrawn their officious vice-consul, and disowned the French adventurers. It may well have been necessary to bring King Theebaw to his senses, and to put the Burmese Kingdom on somewhat the same footing as the French propose to establish in Madagascar; but the case hardly went beyond that, so far as it was disclosed by that first Burmese Blue Book.

The question of the deposition of Theebaw does not seem to have been very much discussed—that was settled in a somewhat off-hand way by the Napoleonic announcement,

"Theebaw has ceased to reign," which was issued at the very moment of the advance of our troops. And a main element in deciding the question of annexation seems to have been the difficulty of finding a suitable prince to take his place.

Theebaw's deposition being assumed and accomplished, Lord Dufferin went to Burmah, with, as he tells us, an open mind, rather inclined to the establishment of a Native State. But, after discussing the matter on the spot, he concluded for complete annexation. The reasons for that decision are set forth with great force and effect in his minute of Feb. 17, 1886. As the communications were verbal, we have not the individual opinions of the officers consulted, and we do not gather that the highest of them committed themselves to advocate annexation. We must now think Lord Dufferin took too sanguine a view of the actual situation and of the reconcilement of the population. But for the rest, there is no doubt of the weight of the considerations urged in the minute and of the extreme difficulties in the way of any other course than that which he adopted, on the assumption that the overthrow of the existing Government and the removal of Theebaw were inevitable. Certainly, in circumstances such as those which existed in Burmah, the establishment of a Prince of our selection under our protection has almost always resulted in failure.

The thing, then, is done, and we must hope for the best. I am afraid there can be no doubt that there is a popular resistance to our rule, such as we have never experienced in India. We can only hope that this will abate in time. There is nothing succeeds like success; and the expediency of the annexation of Upper Burmah must be judged by its ultimate success or failure—the moral question of the coercion "of people struggling to be free" apart. I confess I am very little sanguine that the country will pay for many a long year, if ever it does.

The discouraging thing seems to be the indisposition of the people to serve us, or, at all events, to do so courageously and efficiently. That drawback we seem to experience still in Lower Burmah, after upwards of thirty years' rule. We have never succeeded in raising Burmese soldiers, and in the recent troubles in Lower Burmah the Burmese armed police seem to have notably failed. It looks as if we must maintain not only a foreign military garrison drawn from India, but also a foreign police. A country must be administered under great disadvantages if that state of things continues.

Then, in addition to Burmah proper, we have all round, on every side, east, north, and west, a great variety of independent or semi-independent hill tribes—some savage, some more or less civilised, but all evidently exceedingly troublesome. I have a very painful experience of the peoples between eastern India and Burmah—for some years a large portion of my time was occupied in dealing with them; and I desire to express the opinion that, with Burmah a permanent British possession, we must eventually bring under complete control the whole of the intermediate country. It is better and cheaper to do that, when the tribes form an enclave in British possessions surrounding them on all sides, than to have them raiding and giving infinite trouble on the whole of the very extended frontiers of British districts, exposed to them while they remain independent. That is my experience. The thing is not to be done at a blow; but by a mixture of force and judicious diplomacy we can generally, in the end, by gradual steps, bring them under efficient control. This once done, they generally do not give further trouble. Nothing can be more satisfactory than the present position of some of the tribes in the hill country between Assam and Cachar and Sylhet—to a great degree self-governing and yet quite under control. The Khassyahs enjoy their free elective institutions with Europeans in their midst, for whom they readily work. I myself very quietly annexed the Garo country, into which neither Hindu nor Mahommedan had penetrated, and till lately a blank on our maps, and the result seems to be quite successful. We have made a considerable impression on the hill tribes east of Chittagong, towards Burmah, and still more on the collection of tribes whom we call "Nagas," occupying the hill country between Upper Assam and Burmah. Our officers have just penetrated in a peaceful way from the extreme upper end of the Assam valley eastward to the upper tributaries of the Irawaddy. Unfortunately, in the course of these advances, we have lost some very valuable lives; but the work is done, nevertheless. Our British officers have never shown to more advantage than in the difficult and risky dealings with these wild tribes. The southern border of Assam is now well protected, and I hope that, as the work proceeds, the Burmese border also may be reached and pacified. But still, when we look at the map, we shall see that, all this wild territory included, the annexation of Burmah is a very large thing indeed. Roads and communications we shall, no doubt, open between India and Upper Burmah. Supposing Upper Burmah thus, in a way, united to India, there will still remain the external frontier to the north and east towards China and Tonquin. We must draw a line somewhere in that direction—a task which is an important part of the Burmese administration.

It may be that some day the country between Assam and India will give a great new field for tea, coffee, and cinchona planting, and other European industries, if we can arrange that those ventures should be combined with due protection of the natives, and respect for their rights, their interest in the land and their autonomous institutions.

As regards trade, it seems doubtful how far great expectations will be fulfilled. We already had a great deal of the trade of Upper Burmah, and we know that the present population of that country is not very great. Teak forests will, no doubt, be more largely available, but they may be worked out. Ruby mines and the other minerals may or may not be large sources of wealth. One thing must be said plainly, and that is that the idea of a great trade route into inner China by way of upper Burmah is a delusion maintained in spite of geography and the plainest warnings of the most competent men. The physical obstacles to communication between Bhamo and the Chinese province of Yunnan are enormous. It is I think conclusively shown that if ever there is a good route from our possessions to that province, it must be from lower Burmah or Tenasserim through the Siamese country and along the rivers which flow in the borderland between the tribes tributary to Burmah and to Tonquin. As to the much greater and richer Chinese province of Sechuen, the map shows that it is far too distant, and too much cut off by mountains from Burmah, to be accessible that way. In fact, Upper Assam is much nearer to Sechuen than Burmah. If political difficulties were removed, engineering skill might make a practicable route that way; but after all probably the easiest route from the sea to Sechuen will always be by way of the Yang-tse-kiang River. The physical difficulties, and the intervening wild tribes, make very doubtful the interesting and important question whether Chinese emigration may take place by the inland route in the direction of Burmah, and we may eventually have a large Chinese population there. If it should be so, the result will be very interesting and important in many ways; that might radically change the situation both in an industrial and a political sense; but we can hardly look so far ahead at present.

Supposing, then, Burmah and its dependencies to be fully reduced into our possession or suzerainty, let us take stock of the situation. Having completely occupied the great (so-called) peninsula of India we have advanced into that other great peninsula, almost as prominent on the map of Asia, which we call Indo-China, for want of a better name, though the people are in no degree Indians. Of that Indo-Chinese peninsula we shall have occupied the whole of the western part from Assam and the Chinese frontiers all the way to Singapore; for though the Straits Settlements were originally mere shipping and trading stations, we have now, by extending complete British control over the Malay States of the farther southern peninsula, made that a protected British possession—another recent advance. The French occupy or claim the whole of the eastern portion of the great peninsula, from China to Saigon. It seems to be a very unprofitable possession to them, and one for the management of which modern French institutions are very little fitted. But they are now deeply committed to it, and if they persevere and establish their authority to the limit of their claims, while we do the same in Burmah, there also we shall be almost in contact with a first-class European Power. Only in the southern portion of the peninsula there will remain the independent State of Siam, hitherto in friendly alliance with us. The relations of France with Siam may yet give us trouble. At any rate, that we should come in the East into contact with a great European Power, with whom our relations are unhappily not so cordial as they were, even more nearly than we touch Russia on the west, is no light matter; it must be borne in mind. For the present the French have trouble enough on their hands, but a few years hence, if they are as dominant in Tonquin as the Russians are in Central Asia, we shall not be able to put them out of sight.

There can be no doubt that the possession of Burmah involves great military and political responsibilities, and, I fear, a considerable drain on our men and on our Indian revenues.

Altogether, I confess that I do not feel very easy about our military position in India. Our army is little enough for all that rests upon it now that we have not only to care for India, confined within natural frontiers, but have great responsibilities and risks beyond those frontiers, both east and west, and dealings with two great European Powers approaching our borders on either side. To add largely to our European force in India and the countries connected with it, would be a great strain on our resources in men, and we do not like to add to the native army without adding to the European force also. Even if we would make such additions the finances are wanting. The Indian finance is not in a very prosperous condition, and it would be a new and unpleasant experience if we were obliged habitually to contribute from home towards military expenses in Asia. Already, what with working our native soldiers much, and paying them little more than in cheaper days when soldiers were very plentiful in India, we find our native army by no means so popular, and recruiting by no means so very easy as it was. We shall have to increase the pay of our native army; if we must increase the numbers too, the expense will be heavy.

I have always thought it hard that, while India draws so very largely on our limited supply of European soldiers, we do not derive more aid than we do from the robust and efficient material which India supplies, for the relief of European soldiers beyond the limits of India. Of late years, no doubt, a few thousand native troops have been brought as far as Egypt and the Mediterranean, but the number of those *corps d'élite* which are fit to meet European troops is so small that we are obliged to resort a good deal to the stage fashion of marching the same men round, over and over again. We cannot use this limited force in this way too often; if we are to do so, and to raise the numbers to a force which would be deemed considerable in Europe, we shall have largely to modify the conditions of service, and largely to increase the pay as well as the numbers of our native army. Our best native troops will hardly be content if they alone are too often to bear the brunt of what might be expected of the whole native army, and to encounter too often sea voyages and hard knocks without much "loot." Still less will they like it if they are only employed to garrison unhealthy places which European troops cannot stand. Away from their own country they often suffer in health quite as much as Europeans, or more.

If, then, we are habitually to utilise native troops abroad, we must, I repeat, increase their numbers—recruit more largely from the more robust races—improve their pay, and revise the conditions of their service. Still, it would be, I think, worth our while to do it. We could not expect India to bear an additional burden for Imperial purposes; the full additional charge would have to be borne by the Home Treasury. After all, we might accept that liability on liberal terms, and save in the end something in money, and a good deal in European human material, if we make up our minds to do so. Even confining ourselves to the more robust races, there is a very large population in India from which to recruit. If we offer good enough terms and conditions, we should get the men. I really think something might be done. I suppose that constitutional reasons would prevent the employment of any Indian troops in the British Islands; but in all our garrisons and possessions abroad I should say that they might serve with advantage in fair proportion to European soldiers. And wherever campaigns must be undertaken in warm climates, they might do a large share of the work, provided also, as I have said, they are not too exclusively put to difficult and unhealthy work.

I am aware that there are questions of a practical character that would have to be considered and dealt with. When European troops are serving where they get only English pay, while Indians are receiving large special allowances for occasional service abroad, it sometimes happens that they get larger pay than the Europeans, and in direct money charge are more expensive. If things were put on a normal footing that might be adjusted. There are few places in which the Indian may not be had cheaper than the European, if it be a part of his regular service. There may be a question, too, of the political effect of showing native soldiers too much of the world, and leading them to believe too much in their own importance. A system of reserves would be all the more necessary if they were liable to large demands for foreign service. A commencement has been made of something of the kind, but a good deal will have to be considered on that subject. In many ways the question of habitually employing native soldiers abroad is not without its difficulties.

Baron Hubner winds up his observations on India by the just remark that if he were an Englishman, it is not so much the Russians who would disturb him—"The internal policy to be pursued in India is the subject that would absorb my attention." So think I; and if I can only here make a few general observations on that subject, it is not because I do not think it all-important, but because, as I have already said, it is too large to treat otherwise than by itself.

I have said that, so far, British rule in India has been mutually beneficial to the governors and the governed. We have found in the Indian services a great outlet for the class of young men whom I described as a specially abundant product of the British Isles, and a field in which they have shown their best qualities to the best advantage. And though we have in no degree colonised the country, nor even at all settled there (as we or our European predecessors have more or less settled in most of the Crown Colonies), in industrial pursuits also a good many of the same class have been absorbed in India. Besides the professions in the Presidency towns and seats of government, we have indigo planters, and recently more numerous tea and coffee and cinchona planters. Then we have found in India a splendid outlet for our trade and manufactures; not so much by virtue of mere conquest, but because by maintaining peace, and opening out the country, we have made a market, which we have chiefly been able to seize, and in respect of which we have been able to insist on the utmost development of those free-trade principles which the free Colonies absolutely reject, and even most Crown Colonies successfully resist. Our cotton goods have an immense market in India, displacing the great indigenous textile industry, and iron manufactures and many others swell the total. On the other hand, on an even greater scale, India supplies us with raw produce, fibres, and other materials for our manufactures, and food, too—rice and wheat.

India, too, it must be added pays her own way; the debts she has incurred are on Indian credit and are not guaranteed by the British taxpayer. Except on rare occasions in which European interests are concerned, Britain contributes nothing to the cost of holding India; the indirect as well as the direct military charges are repaid in full. In addition to the material benefits, the possession of that great Empire in India, no doubt, much adds to our name and fame among the nations of the earth—adds greatly to what we call prestige, whatever that may be worth.

So much for the advantages on our side—now for those on the side of the natives. We have given them peace and security, and that in a far greater degree than was ever known in India before; the more appreciated too in the early days of our rule when the recollection of the terrible anarchy which accompanied the decadence of the Mogul Empire was fresh. We have given them a certain good government. I do not here enter on the question to what degree it is good—whether it is all that optimists claim for it, or how far there is truth in detractions; it will, I think, be generally admitted that our Indian government has been good on the whole. Certainly the natives have accepted it without struggling to be free. Nothing was more remarkable than the absence of popular resistance when the Military Mutiny was overcome, by which in great territories our power had been for a time wiped out. Then we have given them great railways and public works, and an immense outlet for their produce. Without directly doing much to assist their agriculture we have enabled them to assist themselves in great increase of cultivation and extension of valuable products. The hardships attending a transition apart, we have probably absorbed in agriculture most of the hands whom we have thrown out of manufacture. It cannot be said that in the way of education we have yet done very much for the masses, but we have given large sections of the literate classes a very high, and to them a very new, English education. Unfortunately, our own education is not of the most practical sort; it is admitted that in this respect we are far behind some European nations; and I think it a misfortune that the education given to the natives is too much literary and too little practical, the more as the proclivities of the classes whom we educate are already too much in the direction of literature, philosophy, and law, and too little in that of practical work. I felt nothing so heart-breaking as the difficulty of filling our native engineering classes at Calcutta in spite of every encouragement. The only very practical profession which we have largely filled with our students is that of medicine; but unfortunately that is just the science in which our own ground is least sure, and doctors differ most. By our surgery, at any rate, much human suffering is averted, and our medical schools must be set down as a great gain. Sir M. E. Grant Duff's experience in regard to education in Madras seems to have been much the same as mine in Bengal, and I heartily subscribe to what he has lately said on that subject.

With our literary education we have given the natives many new ideas, philosophical and political, but we have given them no improved religion; on the contrary, it has been said with some truth that we have taken away their own religion without substituting any other. The educated natives are almost invariably freethinkers; and I think it is probably one of the grounds of their somewhat excessive vanity that they deem themselves not only at least our equals in intellectual acquirements, but our superiors in freedom from old-world prejudices and superstitions. As among freethinkers in other parts of the world, there is a good deal of disposition among some of them to start new philosophical religions of their own. I can well believe that the Brahmoism of a large section of the educated Bengalees is quite as good as Comtism or any other "ism," but it is hardly better or more serious. On the whole we can confidently say that our education has made the recipients much more wide-awake, intelligent, and thinking men than they were before, and much more capable of taking part in a civilised administration and civilised polity. The general moral effect on their lives and happiness must be a matter of opinion, and will be better judged in the course of farther developments.

As regards the mass of the people, there can be no doubt whatever of the increase of population and cultivation; but the void caused by the generations of desolation which preceded our rule left so much to fill up that there is not yet evidence that in ordinary seasons the population overpasses the means of subsistence. There is, however, much reason for apprehension that, if the increase goes on very much longer under our life-preserving régime, serious questions of overpopulation may arise. Already in great rural territories, almost without manufactures, the population averages 600 to 1,000 per square mile. And emigration there is practically none—it is infinitesimal.

As regards the degree of comfort among the people opinions differ. That there has been an enormous increase of valuable production is undoubted; but, besides the increase of numbers, it must be remembered that we give neither our services nor our capital for nothing. Much of this is paid for by remittances to Europe. The public remittances are now about £16,000,000 per annum, and it is estimated that the private remittances would be almost as much more if the flow of British capital to India were stopped, and the transactions showed only sums received in England. As it is, the continual addition of fresh capital invested in India about balances the private remittances, and the balance of trade shows only about the same amount as the public drawings, to be depleted from India—that is, about £16,000,000 per annum. This is what is sometimes called the "tribute" paid to England. Well, it is not tribute, but it is paid for civil and military services, loans, railways, industrial investments, and all the rest; and the result is that a large part of the increased production is not retained by the Indian peasant.

The burden of the debt of India to England has unfortunately been very greatly increased of late years, owing to the fact that it is payable in England in gold, and that gold has been very largely appreciated. There has consequently been an addition to the charge on the Indian revenue (which is paid in a silver coinage) equal to several millions sterling per annum, with the result of very seriously depressing and embarrassing the Indian finances.

All things considered, however, I think we can hardly doubt that the Indian ryot is much better off than in the dark days of rapine and disorder, whatever he may have been in former days under a magnificent native dynasty—we know nothing of that. Baron Hubner takes a view very favourable to us, and thinks that he saw plain evidence of the superior condition of our people as he passed between British territory and Native States. It may be so in some cases, but I confess I hardly think the difference is usually so patent to the eye. Lord Lawrence's inquiry rather brought out this—that our subjects fear the tyranny of native rulers, their subjects fear our lawyers and our courts; and that the preference in the case of tolerable native rule is not very marked on either side. We have, no doubt, improved the condition of the people, but they are still very poor indeed, miserably so when judged by our standard. Their wants, however, are few; they are not accustomed to other than very poor standards, and they are marvellously content.

As regards the form of government, we have established a sort of quasi-constitutionalism in legislative councils, both for India and for most of the greater Provinces; but the non-official members are nominated, and are rather consulted than allowed to exercise any direct power. For the rest the administration is carried on by an official and bureaucratic hierarchy. Till lately there has been little else, till we come to such remains of village constitutions as have survived, a few modern municipalities in towns, and some local committees for some limited local purposes.

As I have already said, the people accept our rule without any active protest—in fact, it does not occur to them to object to it. That rule is, no doubt, pretty nearly a complete paternal despotism, but it is a despotism wonderfully free from the abuses, the corruption, and the nepotism which usually attend paternal rule. The device of a service nominated or selected by one authority in England, and employed by another authority in India on duties giving it the fullest occupation, has preserved us from gross nepotism among the European servants of the Government; and the purity of the European service, combined with entire impartiality and freedom from personal ties, makes us equally above reproach for the employment of the natives.

There is no trace of that oligarchical rule of British settlers which prevails so much in many Crown Colonies. Some personal privileges European-British subjects still have—at one time they had most inconvenient and unjustifiable privileges; but the European merchants and planters have no substantial share in the government of the country, one or two nominated places in the Legislative Councils notwithstanding. India is in the main administered for the benefit of the natives. If there be exception, it is not due to the influence of local Europeans, but to Parliamentary influence at home.

Paternal despotism above is not incompatible with much local self-government; but the new generation of educated natives want much more than that, and it is in regard to this political question, rather than to their minds, morals, or practical aptitudes, that the educated native question has suddenly risen to be a great and burning one. Their demands take two directions, which by no means necessarily lead to the same goal. First, greater political power by means of representative institutions on a large scale, and second, a larger share of high and lucrative appointments under our rule; or perhaps I should have put the last first. It is really that which is most pressed.

It is not education alone which gives political importance to this movement. The educated natives are of a class who could easily be controlled, if that were all. But it is in combination with the excessive licence of the press and of speech which prevails in India that the question becomes a serious one. With an absolute Government we have imported into India the utmost freedom of writing and speaking which prevails in England, only a good deal more so, for that freedom is not subject to the same restraints which we have in England. It is more like the freedom which prevails in Ireland when there are no special laws in force. There must be friction when absolute and ultra-free institutions are thus brought into contact. In such a case the press is almost necessarily in constant opposition to a Government in which its conductors have no part, and with whose acts and motives it is apt to be out of sympathy. I should think that nowhere else in the world does there exist this combination of a patriarchal despotism with the most extreme freedom of writing and speaking. Radical as I am, I cannot but have some sympathy with Baron Hubner's expressions of doubt and surprise.

However, for many years after this freedom was granted, it did not do much harm, was rather of use in showing the governing class all that could be said on the other side. There was not material for the press to work upon in any dangerous way. The Government could afford to say of too hostile criticism, "Well, it pleases them, and don't hurt us." But since there has grown up this large educated class, with the political ideas derived from free countries, somewhat exaggerated and distorted, there is material for the press to work on, with and by, not only considerable in itself, but more important in its working on others. Baron Hubner's definition of what we call "prestige" is, I think, quite the best I have seen—"If you succeed in inspiring me with the idea that you are stronger than I am, you exercise prestige over me." That is just what it is in India. As long as the British Government is in the eyes of the natives a great, mysterious power, in whose overwhelming strength and energy they believe, its weakest representative is clothed with immense power, and we do not require a large army.

But when the people see and hear that Government continually abused, derided, misrepresented, when all that happens to its disadvantage abroad (and unfortunately a good many such things do happen) is paraded and made the most of, that kind of prestige must be very much weakened. Nowadays the educated natives are becoming so many missionaries of these ideas to the classes which are not themselves educated. Not only every student can say tall things in the press, but we are threatened with that government by agitation which is a doubtful benefit elsewhere. Mass meetings are got up for this or that object, sometimes for good or, at least, popular objects, sometimes for those which more nearly concern a would-be oligarchy.

The influence of these ideas not only spreads downwards, but also, so to say, upwards in a way more immediately embarrassing. The mass of the educated natives belong to what we should call the middle class, but also many of the highest class are now educated, including most of the native princes. Many of these latter as well as of the more powerful and influential people in our own territories are becoming permeated, not, it is true, with levelling ideas, but with that portion of those ideas which detracts from the prestige of the British Government; they are often inclined not to be such simple subjects and feudatories as they were, nor as before to strive to attain their objects only by persuasion and friendly arguments. They sometimes entertain men of advanced ideas, subsidise the press, employ agents in England. Such practices are spreading, and the Government finds those hitherto submissive becoming independent if not hostile. Movements in the direction of freedom have also obtained much sympathy from some advanced politicians in England, and that greatly adds to the importance of the subject in India. For myself I say all this not as here asserting that the system is wrong, but as showing that it certainly is attended with some immediate inconveniences.

The educated natives themselves are very nice people; one cannot but like them individually. It is only when they get on political stilts that it is a question. In mere intellectual capacity they are quite our equals; but I do not think they have the energy and backbone of the European; if they had, we should not be where we are in India. They equal us as metaphysicians and lawyers, but I have alluded to the difficulty of getting them to adopt the profession of engineering, and in most practical work they do not show themselves equal to Europeans. There are many industries and enterprises which they might, if they would, learn to practise just as well as they learn our language and literature, but which they are content to leave for the most part to Europeans. And there is something which prevents their amalgamating socially with us as much as other races do. An Affghan when he is friendly is, "Hail fellow well met!" with a European in a very little time, and I fancy from the accounts we have had that a Burman is soon at his ease. It is not so in the case of most natives of India.

As regards industrial enterprises, the Parsees may be an exception to what I have said, but they are scarcely Indians; they are rather Persians—in fact the word "Parsee" is simply "Persian."

What are we to do about this movement following upon education? Well, that very much depends on the question whither we are tending—do we desire to prepare the natives for political freedom, and make ready the day when they may stand alone, and we may be relieved of our present task? or do we look to the continuance of our rule? I fancy we are not yet prepared to answer that question categorically, and meantime we must temporise. Happily, there is a compromise which will serve for either eventuality, and which for a time we may pursue with advantage without too much committing ourselves. I think we must all feel that the task of governing these great populations in detail is too much for us. We may make our paternal government efficient in the higher grades, but we cannot properly superintend a system of that kind in the lower grades, keep our instruments pure, and adequately protect the weak. No absolute government has ever done so. Something must be delegated to the people themselves. And when we have a people whose indigenous institutions are eminently (as I have already said) of a most self-governing character, it becomes almost an axiom that we should make the most of that aptitude. I heartily and entirely approve of the movement for local self-government.

We may well, I think, say to the modern natives, show that you are capable of self-governing a village, and you may govern Birmingham; show that you are capable of governing Birmingham, and possibly you may govern Rome.

My only regret is that it was not sooner and more generally realised that the task in detail was too much for us—that we did not more universally, throughout India, cherish and preserve indigenous self-governing institutions, rather than weaken or destroy them. We have undone much which we shall have to do again.

And, in my opinion, our present tentatives in the direction of local government are too much in the nature of trying to introduce new and foreign forms of that good thing, and to spread them from above downwards, rather than the method which I would prefer, viz., to gather together the threads of the indigenous system, strengthen and improve that system, and from that basis work upwards to higher things. If we have a good system of village government, we may then group villages together for certain purposes, and thence by steps come to larger and larger areas—it may be, eventually, to provinces and quasi-national areas, united by a community of language, institutions, and habits.

I am not preaching what I have not practised throughout my Indian career. My early service as an Executive District Officer was chiefly spent in districts where the village system existed in good shape. Taking over territories on the Sutlej fresh from native hands, I not only maintained and utilised what I thought the admirable little republics of a most excellent people, but myself imbibed from them the ideas of good local self-government, which I have ever sought to promote both in India and in my own country; for in this respect they were far ahead of us. After the Mutiny there was a wave of reactionary opinion in favour of aristocratic forms, which threw things back. I had not a chance of promoting popular institutions in Oude, but I think I planted the germs of such a system in the Central Provinces. And in Bengal I passed through my Legislative Council with the full assent of the members, European and native, a complete scheme of local self-government on the lines which I have mentioned. But I was then considered too advanced, and the sanction of the highest authority was not accorded to the measure. I did, however, establish a system of local administration of local taxation. And now that opinion has almost gone beyond what I was prepared for, I heartily wish that there may be a successful issue to the new endeavour in the direction of local government.

What I most fear is that if we too much begin with the large town or the great district and there introduce municipal institutions so brand-new that they can only be worked by people a good deal Anglicised, it may be difficult to make them really popular, or to enlist in the work the best of the indigenes; power will be too apt to fall into the hands of journalists and lawyers.

The summary of the view to which I incline is that the natives are not yet prepared for political freedom on a large scale such as we understand it, whatever they may be hereafter, but that we must concede very much both to their legitimate aspirations and to the necessity of the case. The only question is, how much, and in what direction? and the answer I give is, local self-government wisely and well planned, and then left to work with real freedom; the object being to make the people bear their own burdens and educate themselves for higher things, rather than to attain at once a local government without faults and blemishes. Such faults may seem great to us, but the people prefer them to the exotic virtues imposed on them by a foreign Power.

In connection with the subject of local government I would say a few words regarding the Native States, for, now that they are recognised as feudatories, a Native State is really a form of native local government. These States have been considered too, and to some extent are, an outlet for the more ambitious native talent. At any rate, they are an important part of our dominion. Yet I can scarcely see that we have done much to put them on a permanent and satisfactory footing. We rather manage from hand to mouth, as it were, and make the best of matters as circumstances arise. Where a native State is really of an indigenous character, where the rulers are of the race of the people and indigenous institutions exist, I very decidedly think that the less we interfere the better. I would never interfere at all without absolute necessity. I have always acted on that principle. But unfortunately most of the larger Native States are hardly of this character; they are rather cases in which an alien conqueror established a dominion by the aid of mercenary soldiers and battalions, often drilled by European officers of various nationalities. Where the institutions are really indigenous, they very often

—as in Rajpootana and other territories—take a feudal form. The prince is not by any means an absolute ruler, but the chief of a feudal organisation. Quarrels between him and his greater or lesser barons frequently arise, and to prevent their fighting it out, we are constrained to interfere,

After all we have still lurking about us a sort of subdued belief in the divine right of kings; at any rate, our treaties are probably made with the princes, and it is easier and simpler to deal with them. I think the tendency of our system is to make the prince more absolute than in practice he was before.

The truth is that in native times a native government is generally a despotism very much tempered by rebellion. There is generally an opposition, and there are the parties of the ins and the outs almost as much as in our Parliament. In our dealings with Native States we are very much hampered by two difficulties. First, in the capacity of guardians of the public peace, we take from the people the sacred right of rebellion, and we can hardly then suffer very much tyranny without interference. Second, whereas in native times the prince generally comes to power by virtue of the principle of natural selection—the survival of the fittest—our craze for legality deprives us of any discretion in selection. We must support the legal heir whether he be good or bad, except, perhaps, in very extreme cases. In the many cases in which failure of direct heirs and adoption give opportunity for selection, a child is selected, of whose future nothing can be predicated. While he is a minor we must interfere to keep things straight; when he grows up the chances are we interfere to keep him in the right path. In the case of a tyrannical, avaricious prince, or one who seeks to stretch his power too far, we interfere to restrain him; in the case of a weak or incompetent prince we interfere to assist him. And so our interference is always growing. Perhaps, under present circumstances, we cannot and ought not to refrain from interference. But if we desire to enable the natives to govern themselves, we should try to devise some permanent system under which such constant interferences should not be necessary. My doubt is whether we are doing that. The system rather is to dry-nurse the prince by a British Resident. Then, nowadays we educate the young princes. We give them that English education of which I have said a good deal. We attend to their physical education too—teach them to ride and to shoot, perhaps to play cricket and lawn-tennis—sometimes make them amiable and accomplished young gentlemen. Very likely the "stable" of the Rajah of Anglepore is favourably known on half the racecourses of India, and at home he entertains Europeans sumptuously and in excellent taste. Yet, after all, he is but an average man. Government is a very difficult task; in that direction he may or may not succeed. The more he accepts European modes of government the more he has need of the assistance of the Resident.

My own view is that, as in the village, so in larger States the Hindus have a great tendency to constitutionalism of a hereditary character, and the Mahommedans to constitutional law restraining the prince, and that we should develop and improve these institutions, and try to make the Native States what they ought to be—the models of native self-government. As we cannot insure under our system either very strong despots or paragons of virtue, rather let us substitute for our constant interference constitutional checks —give the people of the Native States some of that power of self-government on a gradually increasing scale which is claimed for the people of our own territories. When a Native State was reconstituted in Mysore something of the kind was proposed, but I have not heard how far it has been put into practice. And in other States I do not gather that there is more than at best some almost sham councils, on the model of our councils without their modicum of vitality.

The claim of the English-educated natives to office must be considered in two aspects—first, one to which hardly sufficient attention has been paid, the effect on those natives who have not so completely mastered English; and second, as between natives and Europeans. There is no doubt that under the old system we obtained for our service the cream of the talent, intelligence, and education (such as it was) of the whole country. And we must not now unduly minimise these qualifications of our old servants. The old class of native employés were often men of very great acuteness and great knowledge of the country, and their education was not wholly contemptible. The official system, nomenclature, and higher education existing in the country, as we found it, was mainly derived from Persian sources. I do not speak of the mercantile education and priestly learning, but of the classes from whom officials were drawn. In some parts of the country these were often Brahmins with a good deal of Brahminical education—none were more acute than Mahratta Brahmins; but throughout the great countries of the Gangetic valley a Persian officialism prevailed, and the Persian language was either in use, or so interlarded in the vernaculars as to make the official dialect half-Persian. Throughout the whole of India this was more or less the case. We are so accustomed to the official terms and language which everywhere prevail that we have come to regard them as indigenous, when, in fact, they are Persian, or Arabic introduced through the Persian.

Now the Persian language and literature, like Persian art, is curiously civilised and modern-like. True it is that it dates from before the most modern science and inventions. We do not find recent developments there; but for literature and cultivation of the mind I believe that it is little, if at all, behind any contemporary language. Hence the Persian-educated natives were not only very intelligent, but had a high and cultivated tone of manner and bearing.

With the large introduction of English into our offices, we have not only admitted on equal terms those natives who have ascended direct from the vernaculars (which had fallen somewhat low during the Mahommedan *régime*) to a high English education; but we are in effect excluding altogether from high office all natives who are not thorough English scholars. We have thus only one class to choose from, which, though large and increasing, is not so large as the whole native community. That is hard on the non-English natives, and especially on the Mahommedans, who had hitherto had a large, though by no means exclusive, share of Government employment; for just as the Hindus now learn English, formerly they learned Persian, to qualify for the service of the Moguls. I think we can hardly blame the Mahommedans for being somewhat slow to take to English, seeing they had so good a language and literature of their own, and that Arabic is to them not only what the classics are to us, but the vehicle of their religion. The Government recognise the hardship and evil of leaving the Mahommedans so much out in the cold; but under the present system it is hard to find the remedy.

There is another very serious drawback, in my view, to the English system. Formerly, while the Europeans supplied the governing power, the native servants supplied that complete native knowledge which kept us in touch with the people. Now, I have grave doubts whether a young Hindu who is brought up in the Presidency Colleges, and possibly has a year or two in England, and so acquires not only much European knowledge, but even a good deal of European feeling, is not at the same time in some degree cut off from the intimate native knowledge of former days. They sometimes belong to the class whom we should describe as not knowing a horse from a cow. While the mass of the people remain so thoroughly native as they are, I doubt if it is an unmixed good that the public services should be wholly Europeanised. But it is difficult to go back.

Regarding the claim of the natives to high offices now held by Europeans, we must remember that they already hold by far the greater number of what we should call high offices from a European standpoint. The use of the word "Civil Service" is very misleading. It is applied in one sense to the small Civil Service recruited in England; but if we use the term in the same sense as the British Civil Service at home, the natives are to the Europeans in the proportion of a hundred to one, and more. They may be described as holding everything up to stipendiary magistracies, County Court judgeships, and, it may be said, all the places in offices held by the permanent Civil Service at home, up to the highest. The few high offices held by the European Civil Service correspond to those held by politicians (Members of Parliament) here, with the addition of some of the highest judicial offices. The word "district," too, is misleading. An Indian district is a great territory. The man whom we simply call a district magistrate would in any other country be his Excellency the Governor of high degree, and the appointment would be a high political appointment. The average Indian district may be described as a territory of several thousand square miles, with about a million and a half of inhabitants (sometimes two or three millions), equal to several large English counties rolled into one. Save the high officer presiding over each of these great districts, it may be said that almost the whole of the administration, both executive and judicial, is already in the hands of natives. There are but one or two European Civil servants, qualifying for higher appointments by doing precisely the same work as their native fellow-servants.

There are in the service of the Government a few

"uncovenanted" Europeans, but they have come in on the same footing as natives, and I do not here enter on the question of their employment, which is more and more restricted, and properly so, I think.

A few natives have risen to the limited class of highest offices hitherto reserved—especially in the judicial line—but no doubt most of these offices have not been open to them in the ordinary course of normal promotion, just as our permanent Civil servants are practically excluded from some of the highest offices.

Well, the claim to a larger share of the highest offices must be considered in the double aspect of the fitness of the literary native as compared to the European, and the political effect. Again we come to the question, Do we desire to prepare the natives for political freedom? And again we are not yet prepared to answer it. As regards the personal question it is the case that the most literary natives are not always the most robust or the most to be depended on in an emergency; they have all the intellectual power and ability of the European, but have not always his courage and resources. It is only specially selected men combining both qualities who can be promoted with advantage to the public interest.

There is another question to be considered. The higher offices have an immense patronage in the appointments to the lower and secondary grades. Europeans can exercise this patronage among natives with the utmost impartiality; but give that patronage to natives, and would there not be fear of nepotism? We know that evil at home. And natives are very cliquish and clannish—it has always been the tendency of influential native officials to fill the offices with their relations and dependents. A competitive system may do much, but we must take care.

On the whole, I think it must be considered that it would not at present be possible to promote natives to the very highest offices in the normal routine of promotion equally with the Europeans who do the same work of the second degree. But the time has come when, as the reward of exceptional merit and ability, occasional promotion of natives to the higher offices should be made.

The question then is, How is this to be done? Parliament, some years ago, taking precisely the view which I have just mentioned, enacted that it should be lawful to appoint any native of India to the higher reserved offices, although he had not been admitted to the Civil Service, and under rules providing that he should be specially selected for proved merit and ability. I never doubted the meaning of this arrangement. It seemed to me that native Civil servants of very exceptional merit and ability were to be eligible to promotion to the appointments previously reserved. But for reasons which I have never understood the Government of India took quite another view, and thought they complied with the Act by putting a certain number of young and untried natives, selected by patronage, into the exclusive and limited Civil Service of Europeans, to begin there at the bottom, of course. I never thought that plan would succeed, and I think it is now generally acknowledged to be a failure. The fact is, that the exclusive Civil Service is a device to meet the peculiarity of our position in India—to enlist capable British youth for important functions in a distant and strange Empire, and especially to avoid the evils of a gross nepotism which must attend an untrammelled selection of Europeans in India. But such a limited service, with a monopoly of the highest offices of the State, is unknown in our own or any other administration where the employés are serving in their own country. Even competition has its limits. It would never answer to make all our great offices of State, and all our great judicial offices, the monopoly of a hundred or couple of hundred men selected at an early age by competition and entitled to promotion, however they might afterwards turn out. If natives are to have high office in India, we must at least have the advantage of a great selection from among those who have proved themselves most capable. It seems to me that both the public interest and justice to our great and most excellent Native Civil Service, require that promotion should be the result of proved merit, and not the monopoly of a few young men specially favoured on account of birth or otherwise.

The presence in the European Civil Service of a few natives who have come in by virtue of the right of British subjects to compete in England, irrespective of race and colour, is a sort of accident. They are few in number, and very much Europeanised. I will not deal with that question here; it would be time enough to do so if they were to appear in much larger numbers.

So much has been made in so many directions of the Indian Mahommedans as a political factor, that, in noticing India from an Imperial point of view, something must be said about them. Some little time ago, I tried to explain who the Indian Mahommedans are, in a letter to a leading journal, which attracted some attention, and I may repeat here the substance of what I then said.

According to the last census, the Mahommedans of British India number 45 millions, rather more than 22 per cent. of the whole population. Of these, 23 millions are in the lower Provinces of Bengal and Assam, chiefly in the eastern districts, and about $12\frac{1}{2}$ millions are in the Punjab and Scinde—the Indus valley—chiefly in the Western districts, leaving only between nine and ten millions for all the rest of India; so that the mass of the Mahommedan population may be said to be grouped in the extreme east and extreme west. Of the remainder about six millions are in the North-West Provinces and Oude, the seat of the great Mahommedan Empires—between 13 and 14 per cent. of the population of those Provinces. In all the rest of British India the Mahommedans are only about 5 per cent. of the population.

In none of the Native States are the Mahommedans numerous, except one or two small ones on the lower Sutlej and Indus, and in the Cashmere Valley as distinguished from the rest of the Cashmere State. In the great Mahommedan State of Hyderabad, the Mahommedans are under 10 per cent. of the population; in most of the other States they are very few indeed. Including the Native States the Mahommedan population of India is about 50 millions.

The Mahommedan Emperors of India were (speaking generally) very broad and tolerant rulers. They were to a great degree foreigners ruling over an alien people, as we rule them. The immigration of foreign Mahommedans was never large, and the converts are for the most part either the mass of the people, in parts of the country which Hinduism had scarcely reached, or came from among the lower, least martial, and most unattached classes in other parts of the country. Almost all the stronger and higher classes of the natives retained their own religion and institutions.

The Bengalee Mahommedans constitute the majority of the ryot class in the eastern districts. These people are by no means of pure Hindu blood. They are very largely composed of the aboriginal races, of which remnants still survive in the eastern hills and forests. The Hindu religion had but very partially penetrated into those parts. The lower classes became easy converts to the Mahommedan missionaries, while the more Hindu upper classes remained Hindu. The Bengalees are notoriously not soldiers, and it is enough to say that for a hundred years we maintained order among the great population of eastern

Bengal with one Sepoy regiment, and that when that regiment mutinied the people took our side, and hunted them down. The religion of the Mahommedan cultivators has probably some effect in making them more independent than the low-caste Hindus, over whom caste trammels exercise so depressing an influence. And unwarlike though they may be, these ryots are among the most independent and prosperous of their class. In agrarian questions, where they think that they suffer from the tyranny of Hindu landlords, they may be troublesome enough, but they certainly do not represent in any form or degree any class that ever was dominant.

That description of the Bengalees disposes of one-half of the Indian Mahommedans. Upwards of half the remainder are in the Punjab and Scinde. I here leave out of account the Affghans of the districts beyond the Indus, of whom I have already spoken. Of the fine population of the Punjab proper the bulk are the Jats—never thorough Hindus, and of whom it may now be roughly said that almost one-half have turned Mahommedans, while the others are quasi-Hindu or Sikh. Most of the people of the gardening and cowherd classes have also become Mahommedans, as have all the soft lower classes of Cashmere and the neighbouring valleys. For generations, under the Sikh rule, the Punjabee Mahommedans have been a good deal sat upon and kept down. They owe to us the protection and equality which they now enjoy. They are among the quietest and best of our subjects, a very fine people, but in truth rather the lower than the dominant part of the population. Certainly they are not a source of political danger to us. A population of the same class runs down into Scinde.

Thus, Bengalees and Punjabees together, we account for more than three-fourths of the whole Mahommedan population. The remaining Mahommedans are scattered over all the rest of India. The only foreigners of this faith who have in any numbers settled in India are the people of Affghan origin, commonly called Pathans, and sometimes "Rohillas," or mountaineers. They obtained jagheers in the province called from them Rohilcund; and scattered Pathan villages are pretty frequent in parts of the North-West Provinces, and more rare in some other parts of India. They have adopted Indian language and manners, and have about the same relation to the original Pathans as French-Normans in England had to the Northmen of Scandinavia. They are undoubtedly a very fine and civilised people, and represent a once dominant race. Throughout our rule in northern India they have generally been very friendly with us; our civil and military services have always been full of them, especially the irregular cavalry. In the Mutiny it was at first hoped they would stand by us, but in the end very many went over with the rest, and since then they have not been so much in favour. Even in Rohilcund, however, they are but a small fraction of the population, and elsewhere they are a mere drop in the ocean. I have no figures as to their exact numbers, but I think if we put them at about a couple of millions for all India, that would be a liberal allowance.

The Mogul emperors rather petted the Rajpoots, and a few Rajpoot villages in northern India turned Mahommedan, but these are very few. Throughout the North-West Provinces there are scattered villages in which the upper proprietary class are Mahommedan. There are also a good many Mahommedan weavers and other artists, the butchers, and a considerable loose population of the towns and bazaars, whom the easy proselytism of the Mahommedans has from time to time attracted. There are a good many commercial Mahommedans in the town of Bombay and its neighbourhood, and some of Tippoo's converts in the Madras districts. The Trichinopoly Mahommedans used to supply troopers to the Madras cavalry.

Bearing in mind, then, that the vast majority of the Mahommedans are the quiet ryots of Bengal and the Punjab, and people of humble grade in other parts of India, I should say that, as an outside estimate, we might put at five millions, in all, the number of Mahommedans who can be said in any sense to represent classes formerly dominant in India. Of these last, a large proportion are not unfriendly to us or at all a source of political danger; so that after all the forty or fifty millions of fierce Mahommedans thirsting for our blood, of whom we sometimes hear, may be reduced to about a tenth part of that number, and even these are mostly very decent people, though they may have some occasion for a certain feeling of discontent.

I have admitted that in these days, when they are so much passed in the race for office by the English-educated Hindus, and are often ousted by encroaching money-lenders, they are probably not so friendly as they were. But, on the other hand, they have lost much of their military spirit and aptitudes. And at most, what are they among so many?—two, or three, or five millions among 250 millions! I do not deny that if there were a general arising against us the Mahommedans might take an important part. But I do say that we have absolutely nothing to fear from any internal rising of Mahommedans *quâ* Mahommedans. Even if it were possible that under the influence of any great religious revival the whole Mahommedan population of nearly 50 millions should rise together, then I am sure we should have 200 millions of Hindus against them to a man. And if 200 millions of Hindus, joined with the whole power, resources, and European troops of the British Government, could not beat 50 million Mahommedans of the classes which I have described, it would be very strange indeed.

As a matter of history it is patent that the Mahommedans of the classes who formerly ruled in India owe almost their very existence to us. When the Mogul Empire broke up, they were rapidly overwhelmed by the surging up of Hindus from below. Mahrattas, Sikhs and Gorkhas were overrunning the country. We came into political existence in India entirely as the subsidised auxiliaries of the sinking Mohammedan Powers. Whether it be in the Carnatic, in Bengal, in Oude, or in the Delhi Provinces, that was always the same. Sooner or later we took the country and established the British peace—but it was we, and we only, who saved the remnant of the lately ruling class from complete political extinction.

I am convinced, then, that we may put out of our minds all idea of any serious danger to us in India from the Mahommedans alone. They never can be dangerous to us unless on occasions when religious questions are sunk, and they are united with people of other persuasions for other objects. A religious revival such as would set against them all other races is not what we have to fear.

Now, as to the question whether any outside Power seeking to disturb our rule in India might expect aid from the Mahommedans, I will deal with that, too, frankly. I do not know that there is much more cohesion among Mahommedans than there is among Christians; but still, it may be admitted that, if there were a possibility of a great Mahommedan Power appearing on the frontier, very many of the Indian Mahommedans, somewhat depressed as they are now, might welcome the invaders. Recent collisions between Hindus and Mahommedans are no new thing; but perhaps the Hindus may be inclined to be a little bumptious on account of their present position, and the Mahommedans of the great towns may be somewhat irritated to see the predominance of the Hindus. The Mahommedans of the better class do, as I have said, feel this comparative exclusion from profit and power, and even the Mahommedan ryots of the country districts owe a grudge to Hindu landlords and money-lenders. We know, however, that there is no possibility, under present circumstances, of any great Mahommedan Power appearing in India. Well, then, would the Mahommedans prefer any other Christian Power to ourselves—say the Russians? I don't know why they should. The Russians are said to give more promotion and higher rank to Mahommedan officers than we do, but their general rule is much harsher, and they cannot be very popular in Central Asia. All, then, that an invader could count on, in regard to the Mahommedans, would be the following. To the better classes of the Mahommedans our rule is not at present so favourable as to the Hindus, and unless we can redress the balance there must be a good deal of smouldering discontent among them. Throughout India the loose blackguardism of the towns is mostly in name Mahommedan. All the waifs and strays—those who have fallen out of other sects—and some of the predatory tribes, a large proportion, in fact, of the people who would enact the part of birds of prey in any disturbance, affect in a way the Mahommedan religion, and might join any invader in the character of Mahommedans. There is, too, a small sprinkling of religious zealots, real or pretended, about the country—Faqueers and the like—who might be tempted by promises in case of a partial success. And in certain parts of the country, where the ryots are Mahommedan and superior rights have largely fallen into the hands of Hindus, an opportunity of throwing off that yoke would be tempting. I think that is the utmost that can be said as to any distinctions that an invader would find between Mahommedans and other natives for his own purposes.

Except the Nizam of Hyderabad, there is no large and important Mahommedan Native State commanding considerable forces; and even in that State the Mahommedans are, as has been seen, but a small minority of the population.

At one time a good deal was made of an alleged Wahabee revival in India, but I think it has become clear that this was confined to a most insignificant fraction, to whom the orthodox Mahommedans were, and are, bitterly hostile. The only active Wahabee development was in the small religious colony of Sitana, in the Affghan hills beyond our border. There has been at one time and another some acceptance of doctrines supposed to be allied to Wahabeeism in some districts of Bengal, but that would only be of some political importance in connection with agrarian movements. Otherwise the reforms inculcated are perfectly unimpeachable and politically innocuous. Certainly the reformed Mahommedans would have no inclination to join any infidel movement.

I would hope, then, that we may put out of our minds the idea that the Mahommedans as a body are specially hostile to us, and divest ourselves of all jealousy and hostility towards them on our part. I am afraid that there is among some Christians an inclination to entertain a sort of holy horror of Mahommedans, curiously inconsistent with our present liberality towards Jews, heretics, and unbelievers. This, I take it, is partly a survival of the religious antagonism of the time of the Crusaders, partly a remnant of the old dread of the Turks, and partly (perhaps most of all) due to our objections to polygamy. I have always maintained that polygamy is a pre-Mahommedan institution, not directly connected with the religion. For the rest, difference in the form in which we worship the same God is, I hope we are coming to recognise, not a reasonable ground for discord. We might rather accept a certain near religious kinship with the Mahommedans as worshippers, and generally earnest worshippers, of the same God. Let us carry out towards them our modern doctrines of religious equality, and look at political questions without any religious bias.

A question of great importance in regard to our connection with India has hardly yet been faced, and that is, how far it is desirable to promote the settlement in the country of Europeans, and the drawing around them of those who, more or less, share their blood, or religion, or habits—whether, in fact, we should make ourselves a people in India. The Mahommedans did so; they both settled and encouraged the conversion to their faith and society of those natives who had not very settled faiths of their own, or who were, for political reasons, willing to join their fortunes to the conquerors; and undoubtedly they very much strengthened their position by this process. As the statement of the Mahommedan population has shown, they were able to bring over wholesale to their faith a large part of the population in some parts of the country, while tribes and individuals joined them here and there in other parts. The fact is that they have not only less political scruple than we in making converts, but they carry into practice the attractive doctrine of the equality of man, and the abolition of caste distinctions much more completely than we do, with our stiff social and quasi-caste notions. It must be said, however, that nowadays, since their political power is gone, the Mahommedan religion makes little progression in India—they get only waifs and strays—they make none of that large progress that they are said still to be making in Africa.

In one point of view there is much to be said in favour of promoting European settlement in India. As the hilly and temperate regions, never fully occupied by the Hindus, and but sparsely inhabited by aboriginal tribes, are opened up, there is more and more field for European youth of the upper and middle classes in industrial enterprise. And I believe that it would be a very great advantage if they became more settled than they are in these days, knowing the country and the people better, and were less speculating birds of passage, or worse, the mere paid servants of speculators at home. Facilities for education and settlement in the hills would tend to make them more settled. There is, too, the very large class of Government servants, both Military and Civil, with large families and not excessive means, who find their position in Europe, after completion of their service, without root or occupation, to be very uncomfortable, and who have very great difficulty in providing for their children. If our hill stations were improved and extended, and good schools were established, there would be very much to be said in favour of their settling in India, and there bringing up families who, knowing the native languages and native habits, would be very useful, both for industrial purposes and in many branches of the Government service.

After the Neilgherries one of the best hill stations is Shillong, in the hills north of Assam. The rainy season is much less severe there than in other hill stations, and the ground admits of carriage roads. It is not at all unlikely that in point of climate, as well as of facilities for European industries, the hilly country between Assam and Burmah may offer considerable advantages, subject, of course, to respect for the rights of the aboriginal tribes.

I have myself no doubt whatever that if we had gone about it as the Mahommedans would have done, we might have converted to Christianity large aboriginal populations, whom neither Hindus nor Mahommedans had reached. We might have thus made special adherents of our own millions of a particularly nice people in the hilly country of Bengal and the Central Provinces, and a good many in other parts of India, as well as about Lower Burmah. The Sontals and some other tribes at one time showed a strong disposition to adopt Christianity wholesale. But our dogmatic theology, without the practice of the principles of the Gospel, has not the same charms as the simpler doctrine and more levelling practice of the Mahommedans. The Sontals read the Gospels too literally—they thought it was the poor man's religion, that ruling Christians would protect their fellow-Christians against grasping zemindars and hard money-lenders, and take care that Lazarus had his share with Dives. And when they found that this was not part of the scheme they went back. There is no denying that Christianity makes very little progress in most parts of India.

The East Indian or Eurasian population, except in the Presidency Towns, is very small and very scattered, and I may say very depressed. But if we were more settled in the country and collected these people about us, I think a good deal might be made of them. Then there are the old Christians, too, of the south of the Peninsula.

I have stated the arguments in favour of settlement in India, but there are very grave considerations to be weighed on the other side, all hinging on the difficulty of holding the balance between Europeans and natives under our political system. The fear is that if the European element were much stronger in the country they might claim something of the oligarchical position of the Europeans in Crown Colonies, and a large share in the government of the country—not on equal terms under self-governing institutions, but in the character of a superior race. Of all things let us save India from becoming anything like a Crown Colony as we have hitherto known Crown Colonies. The heat and bitterness lately exhibited on both sides on the comparatively small question whether a few native magistrates in a few rare cases should be allowed to exercise powers over Europeans, which they already exercise in some parts of the country, does not augur well for an early approximation, social and political, between Europeans and natives, such as undoubtedly took place between Mahommedans and Hindus; for there was no Mahommedan State which did not employ Hindus in the highest places, and no Hindu State which did not equally employ Mahommedans. The peculiar feature of the Ilbert Bill agitation was that, I think I may say for the first time, a large proportion of the European officials were in line with the independent Europeans on one side, against the natives and an official minority on the other. Hitherto the European officials have been in some sense the champions of the natives. Of course they are bound to do justice to all parties. But I deliberately say that it is much better that their sympathies should be on the side of the natives than the other way—for the Europeans can very well take care of themselves. It would be an evil day if ever it happened that on many subjects it were a question between Europeans, official and non-official united, and the natives.

Besides the difficulty of resisting the claims of a large European community to some political freedom and privilege, and their jealousy of equality between themselves and the natives, there would be much difficulty in regard to official patronage. I have mentioned the advantage we now have in the system under which Europeans are appointed to the services at home, and natives are selected in India without fear of nepotism. But when Europeans came to be born and bred in India, it would be very difficult to exclude them from the definition of "natives," and to refuse them Government employment, for which, in fact, many of them would probably be extremely well suited. Lately it was found that under a system of fair and open competition, owing to the indisposition of the best natives to go in for engineering work, the East Indians were getting most of the public employment offered to the students of the Engineering College at Roorkee. And to encourage the natives, an attempt was made to give a preference by rule to "pure natives"—but it was found impossible to maintain that distinction. The law laid down by Parliament that there should be no distinction of race or creed cuts both ways.

You cannot prevent persons of European blood from competing fairly for appointments given in India. The fear is that, owing to ties of blood and friendship, appointments might be given by patronage to European young men in a way which would hardly be fair. In fact, a tendency to that sort of thing did certainly spring up in regard to what are called "uncovenanted appointments," especially after the Mutiny, when there was in some quarters some distrust of natives and a belief in "fine young fellows" of European blood, who could not pass the competitive examinations in England.

It may be a bold thing to say nowadays, but I confess to the belief that, as things have turned out, the somewhat exclusive policy of the East India Company in regard to Europeans was a happy thing for India. It enabled us to consolidate our system and establish a Government which, so far, at least, as regarded the local administration, was honestly devised for the benefit of the natives, and was subject to European influences only so far as it was directed from home. But those powers of exclusion have passed away. We cannot prevent European ingress to India if we would, and it is hard to say whether it is better specially to encourage it, and try to direct and regulate the stream, or to be neutral in the matter. Perhaps if any considerable European settlement should take place, the solution may be found in local self-governing institutions, in which they may take a fair part, and patronage may be avoided, as it has been in England, by fair and open competition. Meantime, I would only say that, looking to the great production of European children in India, especially in the families of the public servants, to the difficulties, expense, and drawbacks of sending them away to Europe for education, and to the large sums devoted to the higher education of the natives, something might fairly be done to assist and direct good European schools at the hill stations.

If we were certainly to remain in India, and more and more to govern India in India, I should be in favour of trying gradually to make ourselves a people in India, and would hope that, as has taken place in former days, people of European blood quite settled there might become a good deal subject to native influences, and amalgamate with the natives somewhat as the Mahommedans did. But in the uncertainty as to the future, I confess to doubts. I hardly see my way. It might be a serious question if, in addition to the jealousies between Europeans and natives, we had jealousies and difficulties between Europeans settled in India and the Mother Country—something like those between Creoles and Spaniards in Spanish Colonies. It is one of those questions which can hardly be settled in advance. We must see how things turn out.

I do not here attempt to go into questions regarding the form of the government of India and other matters; but before leaving the subject I wish to say one word regarding the interference of Parliament. We have been fortunate in many ways in regard to India, and I do believe that the East India Company served its purpose in a very remarkable way as a buffer between the people of India and Parliamentary influences. But that is past and gone, and cannot be recalled. Parliament must necessarily determine the form of the government of India, and the principles on which it is to be governed. But I do say very advisedly, after seeing both sides of the shield, that the idea of bringing the administration of India more directly under Parliamentary control, of substituting a Parliamentary Committee of the House of Commons for the Council of India, or anything of that kind, is wild and impracticable in the last degree. We know very well how overburdened Parliament is, how difficult we find it adequately to manage our own affairs. To suppose that Parliament could master and manage another political system quite as large, in our Indian Empire, is really ludicrous. But more than that—too much Parliamentary interference is not only impotent for good, but is potent for evil. In the absence of a thorough mastery and understanding of the subject, personal and local and class influences too much prevail there. It is still true that if India is lost, it will be lost in the House of Commons. For many years past all unfair burdens put on India, and most decisions adverse to her interests, have been the result of votes, I may almost say, of snap votes, in the House of Commons. No; Parliament must give a Government to India, but it must be a Government by delegation—not a direct Government. In the absence of free institutions in India, you must delegate much authority to some body which shall help to hold the balance fairly, shall to some extent represent the interests of the natives, and shall be for a buffer between India and the direct action of Parliament.

CHAPTER V.

CROWN COLONIES.

THE so-called Crown Colonies seem to be the least satisfactory part of our system. Allusion has already been made to the difficulty of governing them from home. There is infinite variety among them. A good many of them had at one time free institutions (for the ruling race only), almost as much as the American and other self-governing Colonies, and to this day some have legislatures (in great part elected) which have much quasi-independent power. But the present test of what is called a Crown Colony is that the executive officers are nominated by the Crown, instead of being what we call "responsible Ministers"—meaning that they are not responsible to the British Parliament, but only to the Colonial Assemblies.

Setting aside Western Australia, which is somewhat in the position of one of the territories of the United States, and will no doubt be eventually free and self-governing like the rest of Australia, and the Falkland Islands which are of little account, it may be said that in all the Crown Colonies there is a native or coloured population much exceeding in number the British settlers, and whose interests we are bound to guard. This may even be said of those possessions which are a little more than military or commercial posts. Thus in Gibraltar there is a Spanish population in intimate relation with the Spaniards of the mainland. In Malta we well know that there is a native population in dealing with whom we have considerable difficulties. Cyprus is almost more a foreign possession than a military outpost. In Hong-Kong we have a large and important Chinese population.

Setting aside again these places and also Ceylon, which is a sort of outlying bit of India never under the East India Company, and the Straits Settlements which were till recently under the Indian Government, it may be said that in all or almost all the Crown Colonies of any old standing, predial slavery formerly prevailed. They were plantations, cultivated by slave labour, and, the slaves being chattels without any rights, if they had (as they generally had) free institutions, they were of the nature of white oligarchies ruling subject populations. Since the abolition of slavery by the fiat of the British Legislature, and generally very much against the will of the white Colonists (who very often are not of British blood), it has been quite necessary that those Colonists should no longer be left uncontrolled, but that there should be sufficient British authority to secure the full execution of the emancipation, to prevent any evasion of it, and to ensure that there might not be substituted for the abolished personal slavery a sort of political and social slavery. Thence there has been in most cases a reduction and modification of the self-governing institutions previously enjoyed by the whites. And the coloured majority not being deemed fitted for free institutions, or, at any rate, not fitted for a power which might make them dominant over the whites, the power of the Crown has been introduced in various forms, and more or less completely.

We have more or less acted on the doctrine quoted with approval by Baron Hubner, "that, where large bodies of natives and a small number of whites are brought together under one government, their control should be entrusted to an authority directly responsible to the Imperial Government, and able to bear itself impartially between conflicting interests," or, as he afterwards puts it as his own view, it should be a cardinal point of our policy "to reserve to the Imperial Government the exclusive control of the interests of the coloured populations where they exist."

But the withdrawal of old franchises and the subjection to a Crown bureaucracy, from which they were formerly comparatively free, not unnaturally rankled in the minds of the white Colonists, made them somewhat hostile to the new *régime*, and greatly increased the difficulty of governing these Colonies.

In truth, owing to these difficulties and to the inefficiency of a bureaucracy controlled by a free Parliament, our interference has not always been very complete and effective, and thus it is that we have still Colonial Legislatures, exercising very considerable power and very much influencing the administration of the Colonies, which really represent but a small fraction of the population. For instance, in Natal there are some 400,000 coloured persons to only 35,000 whites, or persons who are counted as whites, all told; but the Legislature is entirely in the hands of the latter, so far as regards the elected members, forming the great majority—23 out of 30.

Another great difficulty in dealing with these Crown Colonies is that slavery has left behind a hankering after more or less compulsion in regard to labour, which exhibits itself in severe vagrancy laws against coloured persons not in regular service; in criminal laws for the punishment of breaches of civil contract; and in some other matters in which the laws are not equal, but draw a distinction between coloured persons and whites. There has also grown up a system of meeting not only the want of sufficient labour, but also the assumed recusancy of the ex-slaves—their alleged indisposition to labour for hire for their old masters—by importing labourers (chiefly from India) under what is called the "indenture" system, by which they are bound down to labour for a term of years, and these engagements are enforced by highly penal laws. Manifestly such a system is very open to abuse, and it has necessitated a somewhat minute supervision by the Crown authorities, of which the employers are apt to complain, and which has not always been very effective, as is shown by the reports of several Royal Commissions in several Colonies, by whom serious abuses have been disclosed. I will return to this subject—meantime I will only say that while in some cases where labour is really very much wanting, the importation of indentured labour is probably, on the whole, advantageous, notwithstanding the drawbacks of the system, I very much doubt whether it is justifiable (especially if the cost is in any degree borne by public funds) where there is really a large population, and the only question is whether they can be brought to terms. For instance, in Jamaica there are nearly half-a-million of Africans, and the black population seems to have increased rapidly. It seems strange and anomalous that large numbers of labourers should go from Jamaica to the Panama Canal, while indentured labourers are imported to Jamaica from India. One cannot help thinking that if the Colonists and Africans had remained face to face with one another they might have come to terms, as has been the case in the neighbouring States of the American Union. In connection with the demand for hired labour it may also be said that some of the plantation Colonies have shown an indisposition to encourage the independent settlement of the coloured people on the land as farmers or peasant proprietors; they are afraid that they may be thus withdrawn from the necessity of labouring for the planters. I think they are wrong; there is no so good nursery for voluntary labour as a good resident population, who generally learn the advantage of supplementing their income by labour when they can get good wages at certain seasons.

In most of the proper Crown Colonies an attempt is made to retain the power of the Crown by so constituting the Legislature that the official and nominated Members should be in a slight majority, and so able to carry a vote at a pinch; but this is sometimes subjected to an executive direction that in matters of finance a Government majority is not always to be used. Sometimes, too, nominated Colonial Members, or even officials connected with the Colony, do not sympathise with the Government in London, and difficulties have arisen in regard to compelling them to vote with the Governor. But the main difficulty is that whereas the coloured populations are for the most part politically dumb, the whites can always find a voice in the British Parliament by enlisting individual Members of Parliament to advocate their case. It follows that whenever anything is done that is very distasteful to the white Colonists, or any pressure is brought to bear to divert the free votes of nominated Members of the Assembly, the Secretary of State for the Colonies is always in dread of bringing a nest of hornets about his ears, and of discussions most inconvenient in an overburdened Parliament. He tries therefore, by all means, to avoid such inconveniences, and does not offend the Colonists when he can help it. Governors of Colonies, too, sometimes do their duty under great difficulties. The Press, which makes and unmakes reputations, is generally entirely in the hands of the white Colonists. A Governor whose administration is agreeable to them is lauded to the skies, and his name and fame go forth in the most favourable light, whereas a Governor who takes the part of the dumb majority must sometimes be content with their silent gratitude, and has to submit to a great deal of depreciation from the organs of the minority—may in fact sometimes come to be looked on as a sort of *bête noire* of the Colonial Office.

A very great difficulty is the almost inevitable personal connection of a large proportion of the Colonial officials with the white Colonists and planters. They cannot all be sent out from the Mother Country, and have not always been so in cases when it would have been desirable. This difficulty is I think much aggravated by the want of definite rules such as those to which we are accustomed in India, and to which is in great degree owing the purity and success of the Indian Civil Service, by which public officers are debarred from other employment, and very especially prohibited from entering into enterprises and speculations within their jurisdiction. Even in the home Civil Service I think there is much want of rules of this kind; but at home efficient control and public opinion no doubt a good deal restrain very flagrant abuses. In the Colonies these checks are much weaker. Local public opinion sometimes affords little or no aid, or may even be enlisted on the side of members of the local community whose conduct might be questioned. It has happened, then, not only that local magistrates and others who have to decide questions between white Colonists or planters and coloured people, have been much in sympathy with the former, but that in not unfrequent instances they have been themselves planters and speculators of the classes whose interests are deeply affected by the questions to be decided. This is no mere theoretical danger; nothing was brought out more clearly by the reports of the Royal Commissions who inquired in Mauritius and Guiana, than that the evil to which I have alluded extensively prevailed and was a main source of the harsh and bad administration of bad laws. I hope there are not such flagrant cases now; but quite recently the facts have been found to justify complaints from other Colonies, that some of the magistrates and officials were engaged in planting and other enterprises hardly consistent with a single devotion to the public service and absolute impartiality of feeling.

From all these causes it is hardly to be wondered at

that the Colonial Office is not always very successful in really maintaining in practice the interests of the coloured populations, and that not unfrequently Colonies, called Crown Colonies, are a good deal managed by Colonial oligarchies, and more or less in the interests of the minority.

In addition to the failure, in some instances, adequately to protect the indentured labourers and coloured people, as shown by the reports of the Royal Commissions, another fact, of wider range, may be mentioned as showing the practical failure of the Colonial Office to control the Crown Colonies. We know how we have held by free-trade —it is, or was, with us a sort of religion. We have introduced free-trade in India, which we really control almost more completely than in our own islands. But we have not succeeded in doing so in any of the Crown Colonies, except one or two commercial stations which, being principally entrepots for passing trade, have been made free ports, for reasons quite independent of the general principles of free-trade.

Of all the aspects of free-trade, that on which we lay most stress is that the necessary food of the people should not be taxed. Yet in most Crown Colonies this principle is set at entire defiance in the most glaring way. Raising tropical products of commercial value, many of them depend on imported food as much as we ourselves do. In the West Indies, grain, flour, and salt-fish are largely imported from the American continent. These necessities of the life of the people are mercilessly taxed by the local Legislatures, which thus throw on the labouring population heavy burdens, little felt by the richer classes; but to this day we have not had the courage effectively to interfere. It is much the same in a good many other plantation Colonies. Even in Ceylon rice seems to be subject to a special tax from which other products are exempt, and the importation from India of the food grains which are consumed by the labouring population is subject to a considerable duty. A similar system prevails in Malta. That possession being nearer home and better known, we are continually inquiring and protesting; but all the same we have not succeeded in touching the duties on food. Our control over Crown Colonies generally must indeed be very imperfect when we have not the courage to introduce any approach to free-trade, or even to insist on justice to the labouring masses in that matter.

Another instance of want of courage (which I should not have expected) in dealing with a Crown Colony, so recently as the year 1883, very much struck me. It was in regard to Natal, which has been already mentioned as having a more independent position than most Crown Colonies, though its small white population seems hardly to justify that position. The Natal Legislature set about a Reform Bill. Both the Governor and the Attorney-General warned the Home Government that a main object of the Bill was to strike at the votes of the East Indians resident in the Colony. Notwithstanding the large African population, Indian immigrants had been introduced on indenture, and being more civilised than the Africans, had thriven there more than in almost any other Colony. Perhaps this was mainly due to the freedom which they enjoyed after completion of their terms of indenture. The restrictive laws directed against the people of colour had been enacted against Africans, and the Indians who came in, not being specially mentioned, enjoyed (after completion of indenture) the full privileges of British subjects, which has not usually been the case in most Colonies. At any rate, in Natal the Indians cultivated the soil, and became successful traders —inconvenient competitors of the smaller white traders. Thus acquiring property, notwithstanding a somewhat high franchise, some of them became entitled to votes—as many as 181 of them were found to be on the register. The whites became alarmed lest the Indians should share political power with themselves: hence the provisions which the Colonists proposed to introduce into their Reform Bill. They inserted clauses requiring of every coloured person claiming a vote, whether African or Indian, an English educational test not applied to whites, and it was also enacted that no one should have a vote who claimed the benefit of any special law—this latter term being applied to all the indigenous laws of the African tribes. Such a rule is also very hard on natives of India, to whom, in their own country, we have always conceded their own laws on certain important subjects. Under the provision of the Indian law, "in suits regarding succession, inheritance, marriage, caste, and all religious usages and institutions," the native laws, Mahommedan and Hindu, are to be administered to the natives of these religions respectively; and the same rule is applied to the professors of other faiths, or to people of other nationalities.

The new Natal law was, however, passed by the local Legislature. The Governor again pointed out the injustice to the coloured races. But the Colonial Office knew the storms which disallowance of the Act would bring about. And even so logical-minded and independent a man as Lord Derby consented to submit the Bill for the Royal Assent, only remarking that this "cannot in any degree be regarded as solving the difficult question of the representation of native interests."

The result is that the Indian vote has been reduced by three-fourths, and the register of Natal voters now stands thus:—Europeans, 7,596; Asiatics, 41; Africans, 10—though the Asiatics are about as many as the Europeans, and the Africans are more than ten to one. Surely such representation is an utter farce! It would almost be better to avow that we give the whites alone representation, than to give with one hand to the coloured population what we take away with the other, as has been done in Natal.

Seeing the great difficulty of governing the Crown Colonies from Downing Street, and the very unsatisfactory character of the local legislatures and administrations heretofore existing, there has very recently been a disposition to revert to self-government, under a system by which all races may be represented, and important experiments are being made in that direction. Undoubtedly the experience of the southern States of the American Union is much in favour of a system of the kind, if it be carried out with sufficient thoroughness and boldness; of that I am satisfied, after a careful study of the subject in several of those States. There the coloured people have absolutely equal rights before the law, and have votes under the American democratic system the same as the whites. In one or two States on the lower Mississippi there was for a time a good deal of violence towards the blacks, but we have not heard much of that lately, and in most of the States the system works well on the whole. Occasional lynching there, no doubt, is, but in America lynching is not confined to the black States or to black people. The ballot-boxes too are under the control of the dominant whites. There is no sufficient safeguard against fraud, as I very well saw during an election time in those States. Very good care is taken that the blacks shall not again get the upper hand. But for all that, they have votes and equal rights; the whites are not always unanimous about everything, and when they differ the black vote turns the scale. And so, without being dominant, the blacks are an important political factor, and hold their own in a way that they would not if they were unrepresented.

But in comparing these American States with our Colonies there is this great difference, that in most of the former the whites are so far (whatever they may be in the future) an actual majority of the population, and in none are they very far behind; nowhere are they in a small minority; nowhere would they be in fear of the blacks as a mere matter of physical power if they were left to themselves. Even in days when they were not politically dominant, as they now are, their Rifle Clubs and Klu Klux organisations made them very formidable. Now they can afford to give votes to the blacks without being overwhelmed by them. In our tropical and subtropical Colonies, on the other hand, the coloured people are the great majority, the whites often but a very small minority. In the Cape Colony proper, excluding the unrepresented Native districts, the American system may succeed, for the whites are there strong enough to hold their own, and it would be all the better if the two white races—Dutch and English—were obliged to amalgamate more completely than they do. But in the Crown Colonies it may be admitted that at present it would hardly be possible to introduce absolute political equality with a very democratic system; the whites would be nowhere.

The system adopted is generally this: to give an equal, or what purports to be equal, franchise, but with a somewhat high qualification in respect of property or income. The franchise is generally fixed at a point which will admit the great majority of the whites, whose incomes and wages are larger, and exclude the great majority of the coloured people, whose incomes and wages are much smaller. Thus in Natal, where there are 7,596 white voters to a population of only 35,000 whites, there must be something approaching to universal suffrage for the whites.

The system is yet only in the experimental stage, and the result can hardly be known. We have seen how it has been evaded in Natal. In the Cape Colony (which I mention in this connection, though it is not now classed as a Crown Colony) the law has for some years given the vote to coloured people, under a not illiberal franchise which would enable many of them to vote. In fact the Malays of Cape Town and some others have become effective citizens, and so far the system has worked well. Its effect, indeed, seems to be visible in an improved liberality and fairness in dealing with the affairs of the coloured people within the Colony proper. But there seems to be no doubt that the great mass of the black population of the interior districts of the Colony have not come to understand or to attempt to exercise their rights. The effect of a large native vote has not been seen; so far that vote is very local and on a comparatively small scale.

In the Crown Colonies the construction and working of a system of representation to include the coloured people seems to depend very much on the temper and action of the Governors and Colonial authorities of each Colony. In Jamaica the thing seems to have been started on a far more liberal footing than in Natal. The population of Jamaica is stated to be 580,000, consisting of 14,000 whites, 110,000 coloured (that is, people of mixed blood), some 10,000 East Indians, and 444,000 blacks. The voters are 7,443, of whom 3,579 are of white or mixed blood, 98 Indians, and 3,766 Africans. But the constitution has but very recently been set up, and we have not yet any information as to its working.

Mauritius too has lately received a new constitution, but there the concession of the vote to the coloured people seems to have been much evaded, though not as successfully as in Natal. The population is stated to be 8,000 Protestants and 108,000 Roman Catholics, figures which may be taken roughly to represent the proportion of British and people of French origin—say 116,000 of European blood; about 254,000 Indians; and a few of other races. The voters under the new system are: Whites, 3,750; Indian, 295; Chinese, 15; so that the Indians, who form fully two-thirds of the population, have less than one-fourteenth of the electorate.

Of anything that is going on towards introducing any general elective system in the smaller West Indian and other Colonies we have as yet very little information. In British Guiana the Legislature still consists of the old Court of Policy, the elected members of which practically represent the planters only.

Ceylon, and the Straits Settlements, and some other Colonies are on the Indian system, the Legislature consisting of official and nominated members only, without elective representation in the central Government; though Ceylon, at any rate, seems to have well-developed local institutions. It is really more favourable to a coloured population that the Councils should be wholly nominated than that they should be partly elected, if the elected members practically represent the whites only.

CHAPTER VI.

TERRITORIAL CHARTERED COMPANIES.

To the Crown Colonies must now be added a new or renewed development—territorial extensions by Joint Stock Companies. After all, the East India Company's dominion was a sort of accident. The Company was incorporated by charter for commercial, not for territorial purposes. But our Government does not seem to have had the same objection to territorial acquisitions at the risk of Companies (though under the British flag and protection) as to direct extensions immediately under the Crown. A little time ago the world was somewhat surprised by the grant of a charter to the British North Borneo Company, with direct licence to take and hold territory in Borneo and to add to their possessions when they could. And that Company has since continued to hold a dominion nominally large, and to govern the settlements they really possess with all the attributes of sovereign power, after the manner of the East India Company.

The Germans seem to have followed the example, and to seek to acquire Colonies in the same way. And now, again, a British charter has been granted to the "National African Company, Limited," which is understood to have acquired large territories in West Africa, in the region of the Niger. Whatever has been done, it has been done very quietly, and we have curiously little information about it. But there seems no doubt that great British extensions and developments have recently taken place in that part of Africa, as, in fact, the charter of the company in general terms states. That charter, after reciting the original commercial character of the Joint Stock Company, and the assertion made by them that they have bought up the interests of all European traders in this region of the Niger, and are "now the sole European traders there," further states that the kings, chiefs, and peoples of various territories in the basin of the Niger, recognising the virtues of the Company, have ceded the whole of their respective territories to the said Company. And Her Majesty then authorises the Company to hold and retain the said territories, with all the rights, authorities, and powers necessary for the purposes of government, preservation of public order, "or otherwise;" also to acquire by all lawful means other territories in the same regions. They are to fly a British flag, to administer justice, and to exercise sovereign powers as defined, or rather left wholly undefined and unlimited. It is a very large order indeed. I doubt if the poor old East India Company, in its palmiest day, ever had such unrestrained and unlimited powers and such a *carte blanche*, by direct permission of the Crown, to acquire as much territory as they could. Then the East India Company had for a time a complete monopoly of trade, and when that came to an end they ceased to trade in India, whereas the new companies combine trade and government. In spite of the assertion of the African Company that they are now the sole European traders, there is in their charter a provision against monopoly. The North Borneo Company's territory seems to have little to tempt rival traders. That Company seems to seek rather to develop their territory by their operations than to find large resources ready-made. But in the case of a trading company occupying and governing large territories on a great artery of commerce like the Niger, leading to most important countries and great populations in the interior of Africa, it is hard to see how their character of absolute rulers is very compatible with equal freedom to rival traders, especially when they formally assert that they have bought out all other traders. Accordingly, it is not surprising that complaints are already heard that the Company use their powers to establish a practical monopoly.

I must say I think these recent new developments in the way of Chartered Territorial Companies are a very serious matter requiring much consideration. And I greatly doubt whether it is justifiable that such a step as the establishment of this African Company should have been taken by the Executive Government on its own authority without any sanction of Parliament, and without even any communication to, or the vouchsafing any information whatever to Parliament. We might find ourselves some day with an African Empire on our hands, for which, or the suffering the growth of which, our representatives are in no way responsible—an Empire, perhaps, as complicated as India, without the resources of India, and without the isolation from other Powers which so long facilitated our rule in India. At any rate, if we are to establish a great rule in Africa, we should know it and regulate it.

CHAPTER VII.

PROTECTORATES.

In addition to the recognised British Colonies, we have what are now called "Protectorates," though the meaning of that term is very undefined and elastic. The primary meaning seems to be that some chief or tribe formally accepts a sort of British suzerainty (but, again, what is suzerainty?) on condition of protection from external aggression, as in the case of some "Protected States" in India; with this difference, that, whereas in India the protection afforded was generally against aggressive native powers, our Oceanic protections are generally against the aggressions of enterprising Europeans. In a good many cases we seem to impose our protection without any formal consent of the natives asked or given. And we still in these days assume the right technically to annex to the dominions of the British Crown, by the mere planting of a flag (and that without even the authority of the Pope), new and unexplored countries, assumed to be uncivilised and savage. This is done partly to forestall other European Powers and establish our prior claims, and partly to give us jurisdiction over British and other European adventurers on the coast. This last is the main justification of these proceedings. It is often a very difficult question whether it is the least evil to leave these people to themselves—to let them fight it out with the natives, and let the natives defend themselves in their own way—or to let ourselves be dragged by irresponsible adventurers into annexations and responsibilities which we have not voluntarily and deliberately undertaken.

The so-called Protectorates vary infinitely, from almost

complete British dominion to the most shadowy claims, founded on the planting of a flag on the shores of wholly unknown regions; but they have a general tendency to mature and ripen towards annexation.

In South Africa we have a good many Protectorates. Beyond the proper eastern boundary of the Cape Colony the various tribes of Kaffraria are nearly reduced to the position of British subjects, and are for the most part made over to the dominion of the Cape Colony. So were the Basutos till it turned out that the Colony could not control them, and we had to take them back. Beyond Natal we have the Zulu reserve territory—a sort of nondescript dominion, and there is still question whether beyond that we are to protect Zulus and Swazis. In the centre of South Africa we have lately made an immense extension, not only wholly annexing a large territory in Bechuanaland, the administration and finance of which are still very difficult questions, but formally taking under our protection some considerable potentates beyond, while our agents have coquetted with others beyond that.

On the West African coasts it seems hard to draw the line between British possessions and those of chiefs over whom we have established or claim some sort of Protectorate. On the East coast of the same continent our relations with the Arab Sultan of Zanzibar and some of the cognate Arab chiefs on the Arabian coast, and perhaps with some of the Somaulee tribes near Aden, were becoming so close that they seemed to be approximating to the character of a Protectorate; but since the appearance of the Germans in those parts we have been obliged to disclaim any actual responsibility for Zanzibar; while farther north the abandonment of the Soudan, the handing over of Massowah to the Italians, and the establishment of the French at Obok, &c., seem to have checked the tendency to advance in that direction on our part.

The territorial extension of the Straits Settlements is still in the form of a Protectorate, but it seems to be one in which British authority is pretty completely dominant.

In Oceania, among the islands of the Indian Archipelago and the Pacific, the question of protection has lately assumed a very difficult and debatable form. In those quarters, undoubtedly, there is very much need of protection against European rovers and "beach-combers" of all sorts. Those seas seem to be specially affected by adventurers of doubtful character; in addition to *bonâ fide* traders and enterprisers, we have there much of the scum of other lands and of the high seas—deserters from ships, and what not. We have not only to deal with British subjects proper. A very large proportion of the British subjects there hail from the Australian Colonies, and own but a sort of secondary allegiance to British authority. The best of them are apt to be jealous of that authority whenever it is exercised in restraint of their enterprise rather than to promote it. The worst of the English-speakers may claim to be Americans, and we cannot prove the contrary. And then there are many real foreigners—French, and German, and the rest—over whom we have no authority whatever, in territories not formally recognised to be British, while the representatives of foreign Powers have equally little authority over our subjects. All these things go far to supply arguments in favour of Protectorates or nominal annexations; and in some of the islands something of the kind has been established by us and by others.

One peculiar form of semi-protectorate has been attempted on a large scale by the establishment of the High Commission for the Western Pacific, with a staff of deputies and courts of justice to give effect to the "Pacific Islanders' Protection Acts" of the British Parliament. But the difficulty has been that, where we have not actually annexed the islands, we have no jurisdiction at all over white men who are, or assume to be, foreigners; while the function of deciding judicially between British subjects and the natives, we assume, involves the necessity of regular proof against individuals, which it is very difficult to obtain or adequately to sift. The Europeans complain that, in the case of offences committed by the natives, the judicial authority is a wholly insufficient substitute for the tribal responsibilities formerly enforced by the operations of naval officers. To judge from the last papers presented to Parliament, it would seem as if we had gone back, and thrown the responsibility on naval officers proceeding by "act of war." And both civil and naval officers being scrupulous men, there has been a kind of negative conflict of jurisdiction, each disclaiming it. The *Diamond* seems to have gone about destroying villages by way of retaliation; but where a murderer was surrendered, the civil and naval officers equally disclaimed the responsibility of dealing with him.

The most notable recent instance of a Protectorate, which has now become technically, as far as our law is concerned, an annexation, is New Guinea, where, by an arrangement with Germany, we have divided with them the whole of that very great island not already claimed by the Dutch, somewhat in the way in which masters of fox-hounds divide a hunting country between themselves. Certainly there was less immediate justification for this step than in almost any other case. Scarcely any portion of our nominal dominion is known to us at all. Even geographers and ethnologists have not yet succeeded in much penetrating into the interior. So far as we do know anything of the fringes of the country, it would appear that the people of New Guinea (or some of them) are comparatively civilised, with institutions, an effective agriculture, and recognised property. Captain Cyprian Bridge, R.N., who has had almost better opportunities of judging than any one else, says :—" Throughout the parts of New Guinea with which I am acquainted the inhabitants are ingenious and industrious agriculturists, and carefully fence in their plantations. Their houses are large and well built. They make very fine fishing-nets. Their canoes are of enormous size, and the trees are procured a long way off. Pottery is made in large quantities for export." The consent of these people to any protectorate or annexation was neither asked nor given; the vast majority of them are utterly ignorant that anything of the kind has taken place. The necessity arising from unauthorised European settlements, and the risk of consequent oppression of the natives, was less there than anywhere in Oceania. So far the natives had held their own. Europeans had gained scarcely any footing there; and the objectionable "labour traffic" (that is, traffic in labourers) had not largely extended to New Guinea. There is no doubt that so far as our own immediate aims and interests were concerned, we should not have thought of such an annexation. Our hands were forced by the Australian Colonists. The Australian demand for the annexation was due to two causes—First, the jealousy of possible foreign occupation, and a tendency to a "Monroe Doctrine," on the part of an influential class at least, in all the Australian Colonies; and, second, a hankering to exploit New Guinea, of which, as a new El Dorado, unknown and magnificent, many reports were current among the Colonists of Northern Queensland and elsewhere. It was more immediately Queensland alone which forced our hands by its action in annexing New Guinea on its own account the day after the departure of the British mail, an action which, though utterly disowned at the moment, we ended by practically accepting, as has been before said. It was certainly unfortunate and inappropriate that it should be Queensland which thus forced our hands, for that was the Colony very deeply implicated in the iniquities of the "labour traffic," to which I must afterwards revert. It is yet imperfectly understood how completely we have, in fact, given in to Queensland in this matter. The Queensland Government wanted to annex New Guinea, and to administer it on behalf of Australia. Even when, under pressure of German advances, we consented to annex, we would not hear of that; we must send an independent British High Commissioner, who would exercise whatever authority was to be exercised as a high international officer, bound to protect the natives against any injustice on the part of British Colonists as well as anyone else. Yet we haggled about the paltry sum required to defray the expense of the British Commissioner and his staff, which would require a Parliamentary vote, and we sought to get contributions from the Australian Colonies to defray that charge. We might have anticipated that if the Australians paid, they would seek in some degree to control. Then that clause in the permissive Australian Federation Act which enabled a Council of the Colonies (or some of them) to deal with their relations to the islands of the Pacific might be construed to include New Guinea. Still, the public were led to believe that the New Guinea executive was in the hands of a purely British officer; and so it was for a short time. But when, unfortunately, a vacancy in the office very soon occurred, it turns out that, quietly, and without any public attention being drawn to the matter, it has been filled by a late Queensland Minister. I have no doubt that this gentleman is quite free from any part in, or sympathy with, the iniquities of the labour traffic. He would not have been selected were it otherwise; in fact, the party to a great degree responsible for those iniquities has fallen from power in Queensland. But still we cannot forget that it was that party who originally attempted the annexation which has now actually taken place. And we are informed that the present Queensland Premier "has drawn up a memorandum for submission to the Governments of the other Colonies, suggesting a scheme for the administration of New Guinea. He proposes that Queensland should administer the territory," &c. &c. The latest news is that the present Queensland Assembly has formally endorsed this plan, and that Her Majesty's Government have shown some disposition to accept it if the Colonies bear the expense. Evidently we are within measurable distance of a possible transfer of New Guinea to Queensland after all, if we allow matters to drift in that direction. We must make up our minds to a policy one way or other.

The progression of British influences, which leads to the establishment of Protectorates and the ripening of Protectorates into annexations, is promoted and hastened by two very different agencies, acting in very different degree. It has been said that the missionary goes first and the trader and enterpriser follow, and that is a good deal the case. The missionaries go out into remote regions without Government aid; in quarters where the natives have little tangible religion of their own, they are often highly successful, and their influence is generally wholly for good. They are not too prone to seek Government aid; indeed, they have not unfrequently established a kind of rule of their own, becoming the advisers and ministers of converted chiefs, like churchmen in Europe in early days, yet without the corruptions and centralised ambition of the mediæval Church. But when their converts suffer greatly from the aggression of barbarian tyrants, they sometimes do not carry to an excess the doctrine of turning the other cheek, and may occasionally be induced to favour British intervention. At any rate, when they incline to such views they are not unfrequently utilised by others who have other objects. In determining the last great annexation in South Africa missionary arguments bore a considerable part. A missionary was in fact the British agent chosen to decide the matter, and who actually made the annexation.

There are also considerable complications due to the inevitable rivalries of Protestant and Catholic missionaries, particularly in our relations with France in foreign parts; since the French, while repressing ecclesiasticism at home, are the special patrons of Catholic missionaries abroad. Our people naturally favour the cause of the Protestant missionaries. I think it must be said that, for instance, a great part of the difficulty of coming to any settlement with France about the New Hebrides is due to the fear of allowing the Protestant work to be overridden and outdone by Catholics under French patronage. And the British jealousy of the French Protectorate of Madagascar is founded not only on commercial and national grounds, but also very much on Protestant influence in Madagascar as opposed to Catholic influence. Much of this religious zeal is very genuine and even praiseworthy. No doubt the Presbyterians of Melbourne are perfectly sincere in their zeal for their missions in the New Hebrides. But when the representatives of Queensland, among other Colonies, go into transports of virtuous indignation on the wrong and impropriety of leaving unprotected natives to the mercy of the wicked French, one thinks they must be forgetful, or expect us to be forgetful, of the labour traffic disclosures so lately officially made in regard to transactions in which Queenslanders bore so large a part.

The traders and speculators are much more aggressive than the missionaries, and though, as long as things go well, they are well enough content to be free from Government supervision, when they get into trouble they are also much more prone to call for Government assistance, and to expect that their grievances should be redressed by ships of war. The best of the traders are apt to haste to be rich. And a large proportion of real or pretended traders and speculators are adventurers of the bad and doubtful character already mentioned. Wherever these men are strong enough they are apt to oppress the natives, and where they are not strong enough they get massacred, and cause a cry for British vengeance. If Protectorates did no more than keep such people in order they would be amply justified. But once any sort of British interference commences, British ideas, regarding commerce, and contracts, and property in land, creep in. Natives whose ways are not our ways are apt to be judged by our standards; people are found to sell, for a little "trade," rights of which they may, or more probably may not, be possessed. British subjects and others establish claims to commercial products, to privileges, to lands, and gradually a set of claims and counter claims are built up which it is very difficult to sift till complete British jurisdiction is established.

It was somewhat in this way that an irregular settlement of Europeans in Fiji led to the complete annexation of the islands which go by that name, and where, under native-protecting Governors, an effective administration has been established, which many highly praise, but which planters loudly condemn. At any rate, there we have a complete government for which we are responsible. It is likely enough that in other places we and other Powers may by similar steps come to a like result in the shape of annexation.

A very important subject connected with outlying Colonies and Protectorates among savage or semi-civilised races is the extent to which we are to permit free-trade of a kind very injurious to the natives—a question which principally arises in regard to the trade in arms and strong drinks. The question of the trade in arms is a very difficult one. There can be no doubt that it is often a very great injury to simple savages to supply them with death-dealing arms, by which their intertribal wars are made much more deadly than ever they were before. Also whenever we are in contact with these tribes they become much more formidable and troublesome enemies when they are provided with firearms and ammunition. Yet it seems hard to debar them from the use of the weapons which may be used for defensive purposes, unless we are prepared to defend and protect them. Be this as it may, the policy of allowing or prohibiting the sale of arms is not usually regulated by any broad lines of deliberate policy, but rather with reference to the difficulty of restraining British free-traders and others from selling arms if they find it profitable to do so. In that case sell them they will. In truth, out of India we very seldom have the courage to interfere effectively; and if we did, we would not prohibit white men from possessing (for their own use, of course) arms which they will sell at an enhanced price to natives. And so in Africa and Oceania the trade in cheap arms goes merrily on.

The drink question is still more serious. Many simple savages have not learned the art of providing themselves with drinks of the strongest character. The white trader finds, however, that the craze for strong drink is there, or at least is easily developed, and that no trade is more profitable than that founded on the supply of drink. Drink he accordingly supplies. There is no doubt of the desolation worked by this new supply of spirits to races unaccustomed to them, and who have neither the moral nor the physical stamina to resist them. Many of our officers, keenly alive to the evil, have sought to stop it, but it is not easy to do so. In places where exclusive British authority has not been established the Germans are said to be much given to the liquor traffic, and them we cannot touch. But also within our territories or Protectorates traders and grape-growers will not be wholly controlled. In some districts we have got so far as, in a way, to prohibit the supply of spirits to ordinary natives. Many of the chiefs in consideration of being allowed freely to get drunk themselves, have been willing and anxious to protect the people from the evil. But the inalienable right of the

British Christian to his liquor is one which no Government has ventured to contravene wherever he goes—so chiefs and white men are exempted from the prohibition. History repeats itself. When two or three hundred years ago whisky was becoming far too common in Scotland, and it was determined to save the Highlanders (then hardly considered civilised Christians) from its effects, it was prohibited, but chiefs, lairds, and gentlemen of good degree were exempted from the prohibition. So it is when we attempt prohibition in Africa. And when whites are allowed to obtain liquor freely, and their neighbours the blacks are anxious to have it and willing to pay handsomely for a supply, it goes without saying that there is a good deal of neighbourly accommodation, and the prohibition is by no means very effectual. Even so much prohibition seems hardly to be maintained when neighbouring Colonists are producers of spirits and influential traders are engaged in the business. Some British officers loudly complain of our failure to protect the natives in this respect. The question is indeed a sad and a serious one.

CHAPTER VIII.

RECAPITULATION OF CROWN COLONIES AND PROTECTORATES.

The Crown Colonies and other British territories and Protectorates (outside the free Colonies and India), though very numerous, and in the aggregate very important, are none of them, taken singly, countries of the first magnitude and importance, that is, so far as they have been reduced into possession—we do not know what South Africa and New Guinea may be some day. In the aggregate (thus limited) they do not yet approach in area the great territories of the free Colonies, nor in population to the great Indian populations; but their distinguishing feature is that they are always growing, while in the other classes of British territory we seem to have reached a sort of natural limits.

While the Crown Colonies have, speaking generally, a fair and, in some instances, a large amount of prosperity, taken as a whole it cannot be said that they are excessively prosperous and profitable, as will be seen when we roughly enumerate them. Speaking generally, we may say that most of them nearly pay their way so far as regards the cost of civil administration, and do not, in that shape, involve direct expense to the Mother Country. It is only in certain special cases that Parliamentary grants in aid are made. And no doubt we bear a good deal of indirect cost involved by these possessions, including the naval protection towards which they contribute nothing. Some of them contribute towards the cost of the military garrisons maintained within their limits, but at most they pay only the direct charge in the Colony, and many of them do not pay that. By the last account the total of all Colonial contributions to the gross cost of British troops, was no more than £139,000. For the considerable military posts the Mother Country pays entirely, as also the cost of the Protectorates which we have chosen to assume.

I will now mention the various possessions. Ceylon has the largest population, and is, perhaps, in some respects, the most important of the Crown Colonies. It is practically an outlying part of India, and is managed very much on Indian principles. It has an area of 25,000 square miles, a little less than Ireland (but the area includes some considerable mountains), and a population approaching three millions. The Ceylonese are a distinct people of Indian origin, who have retained the Buddhist religion, but a large part of the island is occupied by Tamils—Hindus from the neighbouring districts of India—who also swarm over in large numbers, in a purely voluntary way, to labour on the Ceylon plantations. The island is fairly prosperous and progressive. It does not grow enough food for its own wants, but still produces some spices, &c., and is an important field for British planters. Unfortunately, their original industry—coffee planting—has fallen through, owing to a disease in the plants, and they have taken to tea and cinchona, in which they seem again to have good prospects of success. Ceylon, however, has not been, and probably never will be, the source of revenue and profit to the Mother Country that some of the Dutch planting Colonies used to be. The revenue does not more than suffice for the administration, and only suffices because Ceylon is so placed in regard to India as to be able to rely on India for military aid in case of need, and therefore it can reduce its military expenditure to a minimum. Even the very small payment which it makes to the British Exchequer for troops, it was lately obliged to beg off during the depression caused by the failure of coffee.

The duties on food apart, the administration appears to be fairly good and successful. We hear very little about it, and that is a good sign. The people have been long in contact with Arabs, and Dutch, and Portuguese; there are a good many Christians among them. We have now given them much English education, and they seem to be fully as advanced as any of our Indian peoples.

The Straits Settlements were originally, as has been already stated, under the Government of India, and still retain a good deal of the Indian character in their administration; but, a few immigrants apart, the population is not Indian. The natives are chiefly Malay; but the most important part of the population are the Chinese settlers, who are there not only as mere labourers and servants, but also as merchants and enterprisers rivalling the Europeans in business, and greatly exceeding them in numbers. In this part of the world, more than in any other, some of the Chinese are really settlers, rather than mere birds of passage; in some cases they bring their wives and families, in other cases intermarry with the people of the country. Most remarkable of all, they consent to be buried in the country. Even in the protected Malay States (the population of which is but small) Chinamen, attracted by the mines, sometimes exceed in number the native population; and the necessity of controlling the Chinese was the excuse for our intervention. The total population of the Colony is given as 423,000, of whom five-sixths are Malays and Chinese in about equal numbers, and the remainder a *mêlée* of various nationalities. The revenue suffices for the administration. Territorially the country is not of great importance; but commercially Singapore, and in a less degree Penang, are important places. The great rise and prosperity of Singapore as an entrepôt and place of trade are well known;

and it has gone on increasing in size and business, though relatively it is, perhaps, not quite so important as it was before Hong-Kong was created, and other places rose. I imagine, too, that much of the great trade shown in the statistics is due merely to its position as a port of call.

Mauritius is a wonderfully successful producer of sugar for its size; but that is very small, only 700 square miles altogether, and much of that is barren volcanic hills. It is very fully populated, and, in respect of population, may be said to be now, for the most part, an Indian country, the great majority of the inhabitants being immigrants from India—no longer mere indentured labourers, but now chiefly settled Colonists. But the co-existence with these Indians of a large minority (not very far short of one-third) of European blood, who cannot get over their view of themselves as a superior race, and of the Indians as an inferior race imported to supply them with labour, make the administration very difficult, and render the experiment of self-government now being initiated specially hazardous. We can only hope for the best; it must be very closely watched. The revenue is good; the Colony pays its way well.

Though the West Indian Colonies are many, under many separate Governments, they may be here grouped together, including the Colonies on the mainland and all the islands as far north as the Bermudas. None of them are equal in resources to some of the foreign islands, especially Cuba; but in the aggregate they are very important. The total population is about 1,500,000, of whom the great majority are Africans. Speaking generally, it cannot be said that they are in recent times very prosperous; and such prosperity as some of them have is in great part due to imported East Indian labour. British Guiana, in particular, seems almost entirely to rely on this labour, by the aid of which it is still a successful sugar Colony. In most of the other West Indian Colonies which have imported East Indians they are still a comparatively small minority of the population, and they are chiefly indentured labourers rather than yet settled Colonists on a considerable scale. They are generally imported only because the planters have failed to come to terms with the emancipated negroes. It is undoubtedly the case that, notwithstanding all the favourable circumstances under which emancipation was effected in the West Indies—the ample compensation to the planters, the gradual emancipation, the very paternal care of the British Government and people in this matter—the emancipation has not been nearly as successful as in the Southern States of America, where it took place under every condition of disaster and irritation—a great war, in which the Southerners were beaten; violent emancipation, without a farthing of compensation; a sort of saturnalia for a time of negro domination under "carpet-bagger" guidance, which might have demoralised any people. In spite of it all, the Southern States have already settled down prosperous and progressive, and raise much more cotton than ever they did; while the West Indian Colonies have been going down, and are still crying to heaven, abusing a heartless British Government, and importing coolies in a fragmentary sort of way. It may be that cotton cultivation is better suited to the negro genius than sugar; but one can hardly believe that the negro of Jamaica is really by nature more wicked and troublesome than the negro of Georgia or South Carolina. If he is, circumstances must have made him so. The truth seems to be that, under the pressure of necessity, the whites of the Southern States have faced the situation bravely and honestly, have fully accepted emancipation, and made the best of it; while the West Indians never heartily accepted it, have been influenced by a repugnance to accept full equality before the law, and have been enabled by their old institutions in some degree successfully to resist complete equality. So they have maintained the struggle and cried for help, when they had better have made the best of the situation, as the Americans have.

There is much difference in the different Colonies. The Bermudas are far off, and are, in fact, partly a naval station and partly a market garden for the supply of early vegetables to the United States, with a population of but 15,000. The Bahamas, too, are a large Archipelago near the United States, with a total population under 50,000. Honduras is an undeveloped sort of Colony, of which wood-cutting is the principal industry. Barbadoes is thickly populated, and the blacks there are said to be much better and in a better position than in the other Colonies. Trinidad has a large Indian population, and is understood to be in some respects in better case than most of the Islands. British Guiana has a very large area, but most of it is scarcely known, and the population of the known and cultivated part hardly exceeds a quarter of a million. Everything has been done for the West Indies that could be done consistently with our free-trade principles. Very experienced Governors have been sent and various new industries have been suggested. In some instances, at least, things seem to be looking better. Necessity has at last induced the planters in some of the Islands to abandon their dislike to the acquisition of land by the blacks and their combination in some cases to prevent it. The last accounts from Jamaica (which, with its population of near 600,000, is quite the most important of these Colonies) are very encouraging. It appears that there has now sprung up a large class of negro peasant proprietors, and that the desire to own land has very largely developed among the people in a way which is likely to lead to the independence and thrift attending peasant proprietorship. In fact, I understand a large proportion of the blacks of Jamaica now own or rent land.

St. Lucia seems to have a large number of freeholders, and we are told that in Trinidad, Tobago, Grenada, Montserrat, Nevis, and Dominica there are many native cultivators, either as proprietors or as renters on shares—the equivalent of the *métayer* system, which also prevails in the United States.

The blacks of the West Indies are Christians, and a good deal seems to have been done to educate and civilise them. With the exception of some Imperial aid to the smaller Islands, the West Indies pay their own way by the aid of the very objectionable food taxes, for which no substitute has yet been found, and the effect of which is to put the weight of taxation on the poorer classes. There was question of substituting a land tax in Jamaica, but whereas in Switzerland they are introducing a progressive taxation, the rate increasing with the amount of property or income, in Jamaica it was proposed to adopt a sort of inversion of this system, the rate to be heavier on the smaller properties, and decreasing as they increased up to the properties of the large planters. That would not be at all tolerable. Evidently there are a good many things to be settled yet under the new constitution of Jamaica.

Both administratively and financially the West Indies labour under great disadvantage in the great number of different Governments and the great variety in their constitutions, some being proper Crown Colonies, while others have the remains of old constitutions. It would seem to be desirable that they should be re-grouped and re-constituted in a more systematic way, and put under a larger Government or Governments, as Mr. C. S. Salmon proposes, though whether they are in a position to be entrusted with as much self-government as he would give them is a question. We must always remember our duty of protecting the coloured races.

We know by a long and sad experience what a terrible trouble and great expense our South African possessions have been to us, and continue so to be to the present day. It would be useless to go through all that dull and dismal story. The settled Colonies are tolerably prosperous, but their development has been nothing at all approaching that of the Australasian and American Colonies.

The Cape Colony has been touched on as now one of the free Colonies, and Natal has also been a good deal mentioned as a Crown Colony with a small white population of large pretensions. In the old Cape Colony proper the coloured population is largely made up of the relics of slavery—the remnants of the old tribes of the region, and the half-breeds called Bastards, most of whom may be said to be more or less tamed, and welded into our system. But in the farther provinces of the Colony, still more beyond the Kei and in the region of the diamond fields, the less-assimilated natives largely prevail.

Natal seems to be pretty prosperous as a planting, trading, and speculating Colony; but of the small white population a part is the remnant of the Dutch settlement which preceded the British Colony, and a large part of the British seem to be yet only birds of passage rather than permanent Colonists. The importation of East Indians has already been mentioned. The natives, who form the vast majority of the population, have not yet undergone any considerable social amalgamation with the whites, and do not labour regularly for them. They are chiefly located in native reserves, and generally preserve their own laws and customs. But, Zulus as they are, they now seem to be peaceable enough. Though the white Colonists decline military responsibility, they are ready enough to undertake the task of governing the natives, and have lately volunteered to undertake the management of Zululand beyond as well. It has been hinted, indeed, that they have already considerable pecuniary and speculative interests there.

Enclosed between the Cape Colony, the Orange Free State, Natal, and the Indian Ocean is a considerable territory, still mainly native. But the greater part of this we have subjected and handed over to the management of the Cape authorities. There remain only Pondoland and Basutoland. Pondoland is a small territory near the eastern coast. One half, under the name of Xesibeland, we have already annexed and handed over to the Cape by a late Order in Council.

Basutoland has a sad history, involving us in difficulties of which we have not yet seen the end. After intervening between the Basutos and the Orange Free State, we took them under our protection, and, left very much to themselves, they became the best people in South Africa— excellent agriculturists, possessed of flocks, and herds, and horses, independent in their bearing, and comparatively civilised. But, though their engagements were clearly with us, in the desire to be rid of such matters we one day, without in any way consulting them, made them over to the Cape Colony. With the Colony they did not get on so well. Certain transactions, resulting from a quarrel with a sub-section of them, led them to suspect Colonial speculators of having an eye to their lands. The Colony, on the other hand, to make sure of their obedience, determined to disarm them, and attempted to do so. The result is well known. It was the act of the Colonists themselves, engagements of the British Government notwithstanding. So they tried to carry the measure out themselves. A regular war resulted, and the Colonists, after great efforts and the expenditure of very large sums, were thoroughly beaten. Then the long-suffering British Government had to take the Basutos in hand. But the war had injured and demoralised them too; much of their industry was gone; they had become aggressive, drunken, jealous of one another. We have been trying to deal with them by the moral influence of a British officer, under very disadvantageous circumstances, and seem to be partially successful—more so than might have been expected. Peace, however, in the Basuto territory seems to have been continually hanging by a thread. The drink question is a great trouble. We would much like to keep out drink, but Cape Colonists make brandy, people on the borders of the Free State and elsewhere sell it. White men cannot be altogether excluded, and so we seem unable to control the drink traffic. The future of Basutoland remains to be seen.

Our troubles in Zululand, also, are too recent and too little brought to an end to let us forget them. Zululand is, as is to be seen on the map, a comparatively small country abutting on the sea north of Natal. We remember how we attacked the Zulus on very frivolous pretexts; first got beaten, then beat them; first deposed Cetewayo, then set him up again; when he fell, first made friendly arrangements with Usibepu and others, then allowed them to be overturned by the Boers without remonstrance; first solemnly engaged the Boers of the Transvaal not to overstep their eastern border, then quietly allowed them to take possession of the greater part of Zululand; finally declared we would not intervene in that country at all, and now, last of all, have announced our readiness to intervene and divide the country with the Boers, in the form, on our side, of a British Protectorate of the part of the country nearest the sea. That is the very latest, and we can only hope that it may succeed. The declared object is to keep the Boers from the sea and reserve a road to the Swazis and Amatongas, the only other tribes who lie between our borders and the point where the junction of the Transvaal with the Portuguese territory of

J

Delagoa Bay cuts us off from the rest of Africa in that direction.

The history of our transactions with the Boers beyond the Cape Colony is still more painful. Long ago, when they trekked away from us, we declared they should not go free, and followed them. After much trouble and fighting we gave it up, and entered into a formal convention with them, by which we bound ourselves to leave them alone beyond the Orange River, and not to cross it. That gave peace for a good many years; but when diamonds were discovered, we disregarded the convention and appropriated the diamond region now made over to the Cape Colony. Since then we have wholly set at naught the convention, without particular reason assigned. We took advantage of troubles in the Transvaal to annex it, and sent a military commandant, who administered it in entire disregard of the feelings of the Colonists. When it became too hot for us, we changed our minds, and were quite willing practically to surrender it. There was really nothing in dispute. But our Government thought proper to vapour about first establishing the authority of the Queen, and permitted an officer of forward proclivities to drag us into a senseless war, in which he was repeatedly beaten, and our disasters were crowned at Majuba Hill. Then we saw the blood-guiltiness of the whole affair, and came to terms. But we could not, and have not yet made up our minds what to do. First we stipulated for the protection of the large native tribes in the territory over which the Boers had exercised a nominal rule. Then we surrendered them, but stipulated that the Boers should not extend east or west, while we left them free to do as they liked to the north. Then, in spite of this, they made large aggressions to the east in Zululand, but we took no notice; but finally, when some Boer adventurers made some aggressions on a smaller scale on two petty native chiefs to the west, we again went on the war-path. The Boers were in the wrong, and we were quite entitled to act against them if we chose; but why we suffered so much aggression in Zululand, where we had substantial ground for interference and great facility for doing so, but interfered in Bechuanaland, where we had no need to do so, in a country in the heart of Africa, so far removed from our resources, is and must remain a mystery. We were under no obligation whatever towards the chiefs who had suffered from the Boers. Besides the wish to protect the natives there was the idea of a possible trade-route to the farther interior, and a desire of the Cape English to humble the Transvaal, and so do something to wipe out Majuba. At any rate, Mr. Mackenzie was allowed to go up and annex Bechuanaland, and following that, Sir Charles Warren was sent to march up and march down again with almost as many men as the King of France, and at a cost to the British taxpayer of about a million of money. The result was that by a mere proclamation we annexed a very great territory—everything up to the twenty-second degree of south latitude and twentieth of east longitude —besides entering into some relations with the chiefs beyond.

The limit of west longitude had reference to the Germans, then in their first rage for extension, and to whom we were readily offering everything that was not worth having, besides permitting them to take a few better things, and who, in pursuance of this policy, had acquired the desolate West Coast from the mouth of the Orange River to the Portuguese territory far northwards. A curious part of the transaction is, that as the twenty-second parallel of latitude just about cuts across the northern frontier of the Transvaal, it is not known to this day whether it is intended to make another change, and by this annexation to shut in the Transvaal on the north.

Meantime, most of the invading Boers are left in possession of the land claims which they had acquired in some South African sort of way, and we have this great territory on our hands, most of it almost without inhabitants, and certainly without any appreciable revenue. We went into the business with some vague idea that the Cape Colony would take it off our hands; but now they will do nothing of the kind. We stipulated nothing, not even for freedom of access; and the consequence is that, wholly cut off from the sea as is Bechuanaland, and having no access except through the free Colony, we must pay their customs dues for all we import, their railway rates for our troops, and be altogether very much at their mercy; while if ever there is any advantage, they will reap it. Parliament is obliged, and year by year will be obliged, to vote the money to carry on the Bechuanaland administration. The worst of it is that, whereas both in Kaffraria and Zululand we have a natural boundary by which we are separated from further African complications, in Bechuanaland we are in contact with interior Africa. The farther we go the tribes grow thicker; one engagement leads to another. Where are we to stop?

The last Blue Book (4,839 of 1886) certainly does not supply any satisfactory answer to this question—on the contrary, strongly suggests that we cannot stop, but must go much farther on. Part of the territory formally assumed by the British Crown—viz., the part formerly claimed by Makroane and Montisoia, the chiefs on whose account we interfered—we have absolutely annexed. The natives are provided for by "Native Reserves," as in other Colonies; but they do not seem to be at all satisfied. Makroane has but a small share of his old territory, and European settlements are being established in that of Montisoia, very much to his disgust. The natives are to pay a hut-tax, as a small contribution towards the expenses of British occupation. In the territory beyond, our Protectorate is of a pretty thorough description, involving control by a British mounted police; and there also the chiefs do not seem at all satisfied with our volunteered protection. One of the principal of them, Sechele, whether of his own motion or under the guidance of the "legal advisers" who swarm in these parts, asks some very pertinent questions. "I hear that myself and other chiefs have been taken under the Protectorate of Her Majesty. I beg to ask what is meant by the Protectorate of the British Government. For instance, a short time ago the police came and took prisoners some white men who were in my town. Again, the other day, some people came, who, I suppose, were police; I received no intimation whatever from you on the matter. I beg you to tell me what kind of a Protectorate it is that we are under, what its customs are, and what are its laws." Various British officers and others were consulted on the questions raised by our position in these countries. Their opinions were received in April last; but the Blue Book does not show what decisions, if any, have been arrived at. There seems to be a general concurrence of opinion among those consulted that we must keep on advancing, and cannot stop till at least we get to the Zambesi. The Protectorate may last for a time, but "numbers of people with nothing to do are waiting to get farther north." "Whether the chiefs sell land or not, white men will gradually force their way into the Protectorate; by degrees they will lay claim to the soil." "Eventually the country must be annexed." Then, beyond the present Protectorate, a powerful chief, whom we have partly taken under our protection, profusely offers us a great territory beyond our present limit, to which it turns out that another powerful chief lays claim. He is also threatened by a rebel brother now in the Transvaal. If we do not interfere, the chiefs, it is said, will fall out among themselves, and filibusters from our territory or the Transvaal will appear among them. Foreign Powers, too, may get their fingers in. "The country towards the Zambesi is the richest part of the territory." So they are all agreed that up to the Zambesi we must go, with our Protectorate and whatever else may follow, and that white men must be allowed to go forward under due regulations.

The West African settlements are of considerable importance. Allusion has already been made to the African Company's possessions, actual or potential, on the Niger, and nothing more need be said on that subject. But we have also the British Settlements, or Colonies, known as Gambia, Sierra Leone, British Sherbro', the Gold Coast, and Lagos, all scattered along the coast between the Senegal on the north-west, and the mouth of the Niger to the south-east. The territories attached to these settlements are very ill-defined, and do not seem to be very populous and important. We seem to be continually adding to them small strips of sea-coast, or small protectorates over chiefs on rivers, and the great object seems to be to secure for the Colonies a Customs revenue all along the coast, and by linking our possessions to one another, and to those of foreign European Powers, to put a stop to what we are pleased to call smuggling and evasion of our Customs system. We, free-traders in principle, seem to consider any bit of coast where trade is free, or at least unrestricted by European Customs regulations, an evil to be suppressed. If we were ourselves in the habit of considering the welfare of the natives in preference to trade at any price, and strictly to keep out spirits and other things injurious to them, there might be justification for this policy. But I fear it is not so. Our relations with the chiefs in the interior are very ill-defined indeed; but we do interfere to some extent. We have to deal with very difficult questions in regard to native laws and customs, especially those which involve questions of slavery, the delivery of refugees, and the procuring of native labour. We have to try to keep the peace and promote trade. In missionary and other civilising processes we come into rivalry with the Mahommedan religion and civilisation, which has gained so strong a hold on the northern part of the African continent, and which in the west we meet advancing from the other side. Some recent travellers have indeed compared the Mahommedan influences with our own, not to the disadvantage of the former. But our position and relations on the west coast of Africa are still very obscure and difficult to understand.

The last Blue Books on the Gold Coast and Sierra Leone show what I should call a somewhat alarming disposition to demand a more active policy there, and an advance of British influence into the interior among the Ashantees and other tribes, in order to establish peace and commerce by force of arms. The Chambers of Commerce who were so active in demanding the annexation of Burmah, have again been stirred up in regard to West Africa; at any rate the London and Manchester Chambers of Commerce have passed resolutions pointing in the direction which I have mentioned; but the Government have responded only partially and cautiously. It is still in the balance whether we are to establish large dominions in this part of Africa. The Sierra Leone merchants pathetically state that the place is only an entrepôt, and that unless we interfere to render the interior fitted for trade and commerce, they may as well shut up shop.

In Borneo the British Colony of Labuan is very petty. Raja Brook's territory is not acknowledged as properly British, and the territory of the North Borneo Company, though nominally large, is little reduced into possession. The native population under the rule of the Company seems to be but small, and they trust more to the development of the territory by Chinese immigrants. The Company naturally give very hopeful accounts in general terms, but no statistics are available, and I can add nothing more. The development of Borneo lies in the future.

Of our paper sovereignty in New Guinea nothing appreciable has been occupied, and nothing is known. It remains to be seen on what principle our sovereignty is to be exercised—whether we are merely to protect the natives, or whether we might make over another great territory to an enterprising company, or whether we are to administer it or let the Australians administer it, with a view to European settlement and plantation.

The Fiji Islands have a considerable area—some 6,000 square miles—but a population of only 127,000, of whom 3,500 are Europeans, 8,000 imported labourers, Polynesians and Indians, and 115,000 natives. But, unhappily, the native population has diminished in consequence of epidemics, which came in with us. It seems to be the unhappy fate of the Pacific Islanders that they cannot stand contact with our civilisation, and die down rapidly wherever we come. Otherwise the Colony of Fiji seems to be doing well, and, visited by our ships of war, British rule is maintained without any foreign soldiers whatever.

In other Colonies labourers have been imported at the instance of planters. Here it is the other way. Sir Arthur Gordon asked permission to import Indian labourers, because he could not protect the natives from the planters unless he supplied them with some other labour—a view very consoling to those interested in protecting the Fijians, but not so much so to those interested in the Indians. However, I will not here enter into the disputed questions of Fiji management; suffice it that no one can doubt the singleness of purpose of Sir Arthur Gordon and his successor. The power given to the chiefs does seem somewhat excessive, and the degree to which the lower people are made a sort of *adscripti glebæ*, and required to cultivate certain staples, might seem open to question; but it may be the only means of saving them from the declining fate which has overtaken so many of the Pacific Islanders.

Hong-Kong is an exceedingly flourishing place, but it need hardly be said that it is only a commercial station—not a territorial Colony. We have there, besides a considerable community of European merchants, a large Chinese population, including a section of that pushing mercantile element which is said to be taking much of the trade and enterprise of the Chinese coasts out of European hands. Of a population approaching 180,000, all but some 10,000 are Chinese. The whites are about 3,000. We are making in Hong-Kong and Singapore a kind of experiment in the government of Chinese, which may be useful if they settle more largely in our Colonies and possessions; and the experiment is not without its difficulties. The chief difficulty, however, in Hong-Kong, is in the relations with the administration of the neighbouring Chinese coast. We are not always very tender of the Customs and other regulations of our neighbours, and we have not unfrequently treated the Chinese with a good deal less consideration than we would European neighbours. Happily, however, the temptation to opium smuggling and the like on the part of Europeans is now past. But Hong-Kong is a free port—in some respects perhaps too free, for freedom there means, or used to mean, no questions asked. At one time it was alleged that native pirates sometimes found free quarters there, and it is still very much alleged by the Chinese that native smugglers and contrabanders and breakers of regulations find an asylum and base of operations there. They have a free port in which the British interfere with them very little, and where the Chinese may not follow them at all; and yet so close to China that it is alleged they would break through all rules if special precautions were not taken. Accordingly, the Chinese have established a special cordon immediately outside the limits of the Colony to watch and overhaul all native vessels visiting Hong-Kong, and enforce the Chinese regulations before they can get out. This is called the blockade of Hong-Kong, and is much resented by the Colonial community. It is difficult to see how the matter can be settled when we have a great free port, and a very pushing community impatient of Chinese control so near the Chinese Coast.

Of Port Hamilton, to the north of the Chinese seas, very little is known, and nothing need be here said, except that it is believed to have been a mere naval station for precautionary and strategical purposes, and that it is now, it appears, to be shortly abandoned.

In regard to our Mediterranean possessions, it is only necessary to observe that no one would think of desiring to have them merely as Colonies. They are military and naval stations. Gibraltar, Malta, Cyprus, and Aden—and Egypt while we hold it—are supposed to form a chain of British posts, by which we may not only maintain our influence in the Mediterranean, but secure and cover the shortest route to India. I say nothing of that view of the case till I come to a more general survey. Meantime, one word regarding these places so far as they are in some sense Colonial possessions.

Gibraltar is literally no more than a mere garrison town; but most of the people of that town (under 20,000 in all, are Spanish, and we have some of the same difficulties with the neighbouring mainland that are experienced in Hong-Kong. Besides a not unnatural jealousy of the British possession of a Spanish rock, the Spanish complained of smuggling, of an asylum for political offenders, and of contraventions of Spanish regulations. I believe that our officers are doing their best to put an end to all just ground for these complaints; indeed, recently, they got into a scrape for over-zeal in this direction in the case of political refugees.

In Malta, our difficulty is to reconcile the requirements of a great British fortress with the claim to the liberties of free citizens and to self-government such as is granted to other places, on the part of a somewhat exacting native community, who deem themselves a people, and appeal to the circumstances and conditions of our occupation of the island as justifying their claims. We have also to reconcile the claims of a Maltese aristocracy with a sufficient care for the interests of the lower classes, and also the conflicting claims of the Maltese, Italian, and English languages, to say nothing of the claims to recognition of the Roman Catholic ecclesiastics. In fact, these difficulties are not easily overcome, and have not been sufficiently overcome. Maltese questions are always cropping up to trouble us. As has been mentioned, we have not succeeded in dealing with the taxes on food, nor have we yet thoroughly reconciled military government and precautions with civil and municipal administration. The population a little exceeds 150,000.

In Cyprus we are new brooms. The administration seems to go on successfully, an even hand being held between Greeks and Mahommedans. And the higher portions of the island seem to prove useful as a sanatorium for troops disabled in Egypt. The difficulty about Cyprus (apart from wider political questions) lies in the tribute we have engaged to pay to the Turks—enormous in proportion to its size and resources. The consequence is that an island, which otherwise would well pay for its internal administration, cannot do so, and it is necessary to make an annual Parliamentary grant to aid it. The population of Cyprus approaches 200,000, and leaving out a few foreigners and Roman Catholics, they are divided between Greeks and Mahommedans, in the proportion of about two-thirds Greek and one-third Mahommedan.

Aden and Perim still belong to the Indian Government.

They are but barren rocks, hot and unlovely, and involve a good deal of difficulty in regard to water supply, Arabs, and Somaulees. We certainly should not covet these places for other than strategical purposes.

Our latest annexation is the Island of Socotra, outside the Gulf of Aden. It is a barren island, of which nothing is known, and we have as yet no information of the circumstances under which it has been annexed, and of the grounds for that step. Apparently it is a mere nominal annexation, with no real occupation.

I have now, I think, mentioned all the British Colonies and Protectorates which are worth mentioning in a general survey of this kind. The aggregate population of the Crown Colonies and other territories, outside India and the great self-governing Colonies, so far as has yet been ascertained, is about eight millions, or, if we include the Cape Colony as mainly an African population, nine millions. Thus :—

Mainly Indian—Ceylon and Mauritius	3,250,000
Largely Chinese—Straits, Hong-Kong, Labuan	650,000
Fiji—mainly Pacific Islanders	130,000
West Indies, about	1,500,000
African Colonies, including the Cape Colony, about	2,000,000
Mediterranean Colonies and Garrisons, about	400,000
Unclassed and unenumerated Protectorates—say, about	1,000,000

The total, it will thus be seen, is not exceedingly large. Some of the Colonies are well populated; but there is no doubt that, even apart from the need of labour for the planters, in very many of our possessions, completed or in progress, there is room for, and a capacity of supporting, a much larger population. The full development of the territories we already occupy, and any further progress, whether in the nominal possessions not really occupied or in further extensions, very much depends on the population question—

on finding a population fitted to occupy tropical and quasi-tropical countries, and also to afford the labour by which the great supply of British educating and directing energy may be turned to account. Captain Cyprian Bridge, speaking of the Pacific islands, and the decrease of the native population there, says: " Fertile as they may be, they can only be made productive with labour, of which no man can say where it is to be obtained."

CHAPTER IX.

IMMIGRATION TO TROPICAL TERRITORIES.

The want of a labouring population in many of the warmer territories is true. Yet there are great and overflowing populations in the world quite fitted for tropical and subtropical climates if they can only be made available. Labourers have already been obtained from several sources —Indian, Chinese, and Polynesian. We must examine a little this population question; but I fear that we have not yet found very satisfactory means of promoting a large immigration.

The world has already had too much of labour-import from Africa, with all its horrors of slave-dealing and slavery. We cannot suffer such things any more; civilised Europe will not permit any more of that sort of labour import, even if it were carried on in the form of indentured labour. We are too sensitive on that subject to risk the abuses that might result. Besides, populous as Africa seems to have been, there is every reason to believe that the horrible intestine wars, due in great part to slave-dealing and kidnapping for the purposes of slavery, have very greatly reduced those populations. There is room and to spare for all of them in Africa if it were only pacified and developed. Except, then, for our African possessions, towards which forces in the interior still direct a wave of native population, we cannot look to Africa for population and labour in new countries.

But in India we have an enormous population rapidly increasing, and threatening soon very much to press on the means of subsistence in their own country. We have seen enough to know that, under favourable circumstances, these people make excellent Colonists. They are accustomed to agriculture, quiet and law-abiding, industrious, frugal, and very intelligent, and they have also a natural aptitude for commercial pursuits. Yet there are great difficulties in the way. There is evidence that the Hindus were once, in prehistoric times, a seafaring and colonising people, but for many centuries this has ceased to be so; Arabs, Malays, and Europeans have ousted them from that function. The modern peoples of India are not only not seafaring, but have a proverbial dread of the "black water," which the vast majority have never seen, and only know as a mysterious terror. Then the caste system and the social trammels under which Indians live, stand very much in the way of emigration. The better and more enterprising classes do not attempt any voluntary emigration whatever. Those of them who are now educated beyond old superstitions are not, as has been already explained, at all prone to rough enterprise. They may go to England to compete for appointments and take degrees, but they will not be the pioneers of colonisation. Hence emigrants can only be sought among the poor and the needy or the casteless, and not many of them are yet willing to go. Those who are willing have not the means.

Hence has arisen the indenture system, under which they are sought out, and their expenses are paid by those who desire their labour, on condition that they are bound to labour for a term of years. But this system is very liable to abuses. To begin with, the Colonies and employers of labour who want coolies do not deal direct with possible emigrants in the interior of the country. They employ recruiters, and the remuneration of the recruiters has very generally taken the form of a payment of so much per head to contractors for the supply of labourers, a system not only suggestive of a near analogy to the buying and selling of human beings, but necessarily offering great temptations to abuse. Then sometimes great hardship and much mortality occurred in the passage to distant Colonies in crowded vessels, sometimes inefficiently found. And there was little security that on arrival in remote Colonies the emigrants would be treated as well as those who engaged them had led them to expect. Hence the Indian Government was obliged to step in to protect its subjects, to take full precautions against the abuses of mercenary touts and recruiters, to insist on adequate provision for the voyage, and to limit emigration to those Colonies and territories where they were satisfied that the local laws made adequate provision for the protection of Indian immigrants. But then, all these precautions cost money, increased the expense of emigration, and in proportion as it is costly the planters insist on long terms of servitude to recoup the expense.

The machinery at the disposal of the Indian Government enables them to put down the abuses of the recruiters, and to make reasonable provision for the health and safety of the emigrants on board ship. The mortality from sickness on the way is not now excessive; but disastrous shipwrecks are still, unfortunately, not uncommon, and I am sorry to say that on these occasions British officers and crews have sometimes shown themselves in a light happily rare among British seamen—saving themselves, and leaving their passengers to perish like so many derelict cattle. Some of the officers and sailors in second-rate ships seem hardly to regard coloured passengers in the same light as those who are white. Not to go back to several cases within my own experience, take the following very recent case from Baron Hubner's travels. As he arrives at Fiji: "We pass near a large steamer, wrecked a few days before on a coral reef. She had come from

Calcutta with a considerable number of coolies engaged by planters. The captain, officers, and crew, all of them drunk when the catastrophe occurred, were saved, but not one of the poor Hindus escaped death." There may very likely be question as to the sweeping charge of drunkenness, but as to the more material facts, I fear the event was too near for any great mistake on the Baron's part.

It is not very long ago that the officers and crew of a pilgrim ship came into Aden and reported the loss of the ship, which they had left in a sinking state. But a few days later another vessel towed the derelict into port, not very much the worse, and with several hundred pilgrims on board. I never heard that those officers were seriously punished for the incident.

So far as regards promises and undertakings, the Indian Government secured good treatment for its emigrant subjects in the Colonies, but the reports of several Royal Commissions have abundantly shown that in practice these precautions were sometimes by no means effectual. I will take, as an instance, Mauritius, the Colony nearest to India, where the Indians are mostly a settled population, and where one might most have expected that their good treatment would be secured. There had grown up a large Indian population, free of the indentures by which they were originally bound. The planters were jealous of free Indians, who would not work on estates. They attributed to them all sorts of wickedness and evil designs, which seem really ludicrous to those who know these people. A compliant governor happened to preside, and, in spite of the protest of some of the best and most experienced island officers, a law was passed, of extreme severity, which not only led to great abuses in regard to labourers under indenture, but put those whose terms had expired, and who desired to remain free, under such harsh conditions that they were

K

driven into re-engagements, or if they refused, reduced to an almost servile condition.

I will not quote the strong language of the report of the Royal Commission of 1874 regarding the many abuses which they found to prevail in the treatment of indentured labourers, but I more particularly note those affecting the Indians supposed to be free. If within eight days of expiry of indenture they did not re-indenture, they were subjected to a system of the most harassing supervision, under what was called the "Pass system"—they could not pursue any calling without a police permit, for which they paid heavily, could not move from one place to another without a special permit, were obliged to exhibit a ticket with their photograph to the police, and were charged a heavy sum for the photograph, for the benefit of favoured persons, and were subject to other restrictions. Altogether, the terms of the law were such that when it was received in England, even without the subsequent light thrown by the Royal Commission on the manner of its execution, the Emigration Commissioners were obliged to say that "it subjected the old immigrants not employed on estates to a control which in this country has been applied only to men under tickets of leave." It was observed, however, that "the opinions of those on the spot, with the best means of judging, were decided and unanimous as to the necessity for such a law"—quite an error, for the adverse opinions had not been sent home; and so the law was "allowed to go into operation."

The Royal Commissioners, besides reporting on the injustice of the law, say, "We farther find that this law was enforced both by the police and the magistrates in such a reckless and indiscreet manner as to cause cruel hardships to a number of Your Majesty's subjects."

After so strong a report in great detail had been made by a Royal Commission of unquestioned impartiality, one would have expected that not a moment would have been lost in puting an end to such flagrant abuses. But the Colonial Office deal very gently with Colonists, whom they may bring like hornets about their ears. While quite accepting the necessity of acting on the report, they went about the matter very slowly and quietly, with many references and much hesitation. Many years passed before the obnoxious ordinance was finally repealed. It was repealed at last, and much more equitable laws and rules were substituted, of which there is little to complain, except that I believe to this day free Indians are not placed on complete equality with other races, and are subject to some special restrictions under the name of vagrancy laws.

It may be admitted, too, that in other Colonies, consequent on the report of the Royal Commissions, particular abuses have been for the most part remedied, and greater care is now exercised. But what has been may be. I have always maintained that, after expiry of indenture, Indian immigrants should be entitled to all the privileges of free British subjects, independent of race and colour. But that doctrine has not yet been fully accepted.

Emigration from India still goes on, but does not seem to increase, but rather the contrary; it varies, I think, a little above or below some 20,000 per annum. The people who go are frugal, and sometimes save a good deal of money, though I think there is a good deal of exaggeration about that. We have figures only regarding the minority who return home with their earnings; and then the considerable capital of successful traders, included in averages, gives a fictitious appearance of large savings so far as mere labourers are concerned. A good many do thus return home; a good many settle in some of the Colonies; a great many are unaccounted for, and in one way or other fall out by the way. I cannot hear that in many of the Colonies the Indians are much settled on the land. In Mauritius space is wanting; in that and other Colonies such settlement has been discouraged. I have heard of something of settlement in Trinidad and one or two other places; but we have very little information. The whole question of large emigration from India is one which still awaits solution.

My own opinion is that we cannot have emigration from India on a large scale, and on satisfactory conditions, till the Indian Government is able more actively to encourage and facilitate it; and this can hardly be till the British Government more directly and clearly undertakes the responsibility of protecting the coloured races in British Colonies and possessions not recognised as wholly self-governing. I think emigration from India most desirable for all parties—most desirable as an outlet to overflowing Indian populations, and most desirable as a means of populating warm countries not well suited for white labour. But I think it must be on the condition that the emigrants have at least that complete personal freedom which they have in India, and that they are not in any degree treated as an inferior or servile race. I confess I should not be willing to trust them to a Colonial Government, under such conditions as those of the new Mauritius Constitution, where the votes of the planting interest will completely monopolise the representation. I cannot think, too, that emigration on a large scale can be satisfactory unless facilities for settling on the land are offered to the emigrants in new countries where land is plentiful.

The Chinese are a more robust race than the Indians—probably better fitted for Colonists; especially where hardship has to be endured, and rough work has to be done, they are much superior. I cannot understand the view taken by Baron Hubner in this matter; and no one has had better opportunities of seeing Chinese emigrants in all parts of the world. He is never tired of praising the Chinaman wherever he meets him—"active, sober, of proverbial honesty; an excellent cultivator, a first-rate gardener; a born merchant; a first-class cook; unsurpassed as a handi-craftsman"—he has every industrial virtue under the sun, and he beats the white man, "not by force, but with the weapons of labour and thrift." Yet he winds up his summary as if he thought Chinese immigration the greatest misfortune; he speaks of the white river as fertilising the lands through which it runs with the seeds of Christian civilisation, and the yellow river as threatening to destroy them. I must say that, apart from the question of preserving the temperate countries as white men's lands, it seems to me that the objection to relying on Chinese as Colonists is not so much their inferiority in religion to the white adventurers who object to their competition, as the fact that, except to the limited extent already mentioned in some places not very far removed from China, they do not come as Colonists, but only as labourers and fortune-seekers—mere birds of passage. They are in a country, but not of it. They remain completely foreigners, whose ways we do not understand. They have their own self-government, of which we know nothing; their own feuds, of which we are sometimes very painfully made aware; their own habits and methods.

After often inquiring, I have never been able to discover why Chinamen will not bring their wives and families and settle; how far it is a mere social prejudice, or how far the Chinese rulers are unwilling to give up a hold over their subjects. Be this as it may, till the difficulty is got over we must look on the Chinese as foreign labourers, and not as Colonists. We are hardly yet in a position to form an opinion what they would be if they really colonised, and how we should get on with them. But it is a very pregnant question as regards the future history of the world.

The Polynesians cannot possibly be a source of very large supply of immigrants—that source has already been overdone. Very great abuses have occurred, and the practice has accelerated the tendency to decline in the population, already too pronounced. No doubt some of the islands are more populous than others, but the whole population is not large, and is certainly decreasing. Planters, no doubt, think it right that labour should be fetched from islands where there are no planters, to islands where there are; but the general result of the statements of those who know best is that nowhere in those parts of the world is labour redundant, if there were peace and opportunity to exercise it beneficially.

The abuses of the Polynesian labour traffic are beyond doubt—there is nothing in modern times more shocking. They are proved not only by a great concurrence of testimony, but also by the report of the Commission on the Western Pacific, and by recent trials. There seems no doubt that natives were habitually kidnapped and bought—that even when voluntarily engaged they were misled and deceived as to the terms of the engagement: in short, that every offence that was possible was committed by unscrupulous recruiters paid by results, and very insufficiently supervised by inefficient agents. It is also clear that very great mortality occurred among them on Queensland plantations; and even when they survived their term of service, the stipulation to return them to their homes was very insufficiently performed, it often happening that the wrong man was landed on the wrong island, and there probably plundered and eaten. The supervision, such as it was, mostly was in the hands of the Colonial Government, in which the planters, who profited by the system, were most powerful. Since the conscience of Queensland was awakened, and the labour-traffic party have fallen from power, some trials have taken place in the Colonies. In a recent case it was clearly proved that the master and crew of the labour vessel deliberately intercepted canoes and captured their occupants, that when they resisted they were run down, and when the natives, in the attempt to escape, jumped into the water, they were shot without remorse. More inexcusable and horrid murders could not be imagined, and convicted of murder the perpetrators were; but they were not executed.

No doubt since these disclosures the traffic has been more supervised, and the abuses much abated, but it is a dangerous and doubtful traffic at best.

In connection with this question may be mentioned the barbarous system of reprisals by our ships of war, for alleged offences by uncivilised natives, which has largely prevailed both on the coasts of Africa and in the Pacific, and against which some of our best officers have much protested. It has always seemed to me that the British conscience is strangely variable; sometimes it is much excited—it may be on a matter of secondary importance, or on a very small scale; but at other times it is very slow to move. And so it is here, though repeated Blue Books have been published showing clearly enough how, on a complaint regarding some quarrel or some outrage on a white man, vessels of war have been sent to demand satisfaction or surrender of alleged criminals, and not obtaining that, have, without regard to the criminality of particular individuals, bombarded this and that native town, and landed and destroyed houses and crops and fruit-trees and whatever they could find, and spread devastation far and wide. It is a most barbarous system. In the Pacific these expeditions were generally undertaken on account of the murder of some trader or sailor by the natives; and they, on their part, in most instances killed the white man in retaliation for offences committed against them by some other white men, who had kidnapped their relations, or committed some other offence against them. As Captain Bridge says, we, acting on old-fashioned notions, punish the tribe for the act or suspected act of the individual, and the natives equally seek to punish members of the limited white tribe with which they are acquainted, for the acts of white men, deeming it much the same thing. But we do not admit that the same measure applies to ourselves and to others. In our own case we insist on exact individual proof and individual justice, which we quite dispense with when we are dealing with weaker tribes or peoples.

In the Pacific an attempt has been made, through the Western Pacific Commission, to substitute for the system of reprisals individual responsibility, and some sort of regular trial ; but it is hardly claimed that the result has been very successful. There are great difficulties in the way. We cannot control the action of the ships of foreign Powers. German officers have lately reported exploits such as we used to perpetrate in those regions. In truth, we ourselves seem to have reverted to naval reprisals in the Pacific ; and I do not learn that in Africa our officers have yet been forbidden that system, though some of their reports show that they do not at all like it.

CHAPTER X.

EXTENSION OR RETROGRESSION.

WE have seen how rapid has been the extension of our territories of late years. The question is, Are we to continue so to extend? Well, perhaps we may save a good deal of argument on that point if we consider where we can farther extend. Even the tropical world has its limits. There is nothing more to be got in America, and nothing in Asia that any sane man would touch. We have already in form annexed our share of the great islands Borneo and New Guinea; and in the latter it is only a question of administration whether we are merely to protect the natives or to exploit the country. We have divided the Pacific with Germany, and it only remains to come to terms with France. It hardly lies in the mouth of us, who steal so many sheep all over the world, to make virtuous protests if France steals a few lambs. If the French choose to take Tonquin, and establish a Protectorate over Madagascar, it is their affair. They have just as good a right to do it as we have to do the same thing in many other quarters. If we could bring ourselves honestly and frankly to acknowledge that, we might probably settle matters with France—so far, at least, as Oceania is concerned. It would be most desirable to arrange something with France and Germany to get rid of the joint engagements regarding the New Hebrides and one or two smaller places. If the Australians would allow us to come to terms with France about the New Hebrides, we might then probably have the rest of the South Pacific to ourselves, and so satisfy all the reasonable demands of the Australians to be relieved, as far as possible, of the risk of great foreign establishments in their neighbourhood. If so much were arranged, there would remain only the great Continent of Africa. That I reserve to discuss separately. But outside Africa there really are no more worlds to conquer. We might, if we liked, establish a few more Fijis in the Pacific; that is about all. Cast about where we will, I do not see room for further extensions out of Africa. And it is perhaps well that it should be so; we have been going rather fast of late.

If the natural limits of the globe check our going forward, we are not prepared to go back directly and avowedly. We have not accepted fully Mr. Gladstone's lessons on the danger of too great empire. But we are, I think, as much as ever inclined to shuffle off our responsibilities by turning them over to any one who will take them within the Empire itself, if it can be called an Empire. Now, I think it is a very important question whether it is right, and justifiable, and politic, to turn over native populations whom we have made our subjects, or taken under our protection, to the self-governing Colonies, where these natives are not represented, and by whom they are governed as outlying dependencies—to create, as it were, *imperia in imperio*. I must say that I am decidedly against this policy. The question practically arises in regard to Australasia and the Pacific, and in South Africa. It seems to me that such a transfer is good for no party; that it is a shirking on our part of obligations which we have chosen to undertake; that it is unfair to the natives; and that it is by no means good for the Colonies. Surely the three millions of white Australians have enough to do, and will for a long time to come (even when they increase to ten times the number), to develop their own magnificent possessions, without insisting that a few among them should undertake the exploitation of other countries, which Nature has not made to be white men's countries, and the government of subject races—a task which diverts them from their own proper tasks, and which has sometimes a very demoralising effect, as in regard to transactions affecting the Pacific islanders, to which allusion has been made.

It is true enough that in the more settled parts of the Colonies there is much of the same public opinion which, with us, sooner or later, restrains and corrects great excesses, and that when that feeling is aroused we might expect Colonial opinion also to do much to correct abuses. But still, for a very long time to come, the body of impartial people in the Colonies must be smaller in proportion, and the speculative element must be larger in proportion than with us—there is not the same enormous middle class. And at any rate, I come back to this, that the Colonists have enough to do at home; that they can only operate abroad under the protection of a navy and a foreign diplomacy; and that while we claim to be one Empire we can have only one navy, and one diplomacy on the high seas. All the Colonies are not equally settled. However it may be in future days when they are more ripe and more settled, I do not think that we can advantageously turn over native populations to them at present, especially when the consent of those natives is neither asked nor given. Yet I am afraid it is in that direction that our policy is tending. The clause in the Australian Federation Act about the Pacific, the inclusion of the Crown Colony of Fiji in that arrangement, the demand for pecuniary contributions from the Colonies for the management of New Guinea, the appointment of a Queenslander to be commissioner for New Guinea, and all we hear of plans for the administration of New Guinea by Queensland, on the part of the Australian Colonies—all these things seem to point in the same direction. I must say that in my opinion to make over New Guinea to Queensland would be a base and unjustifiable policy. Without reverting more to questions connected with the labour traffic and the Australian aborigines, I must recall Captain Bridge's description of the civilised self-governing character, and agricultural and manufacturing capacities of the natives of New Guinea. These people should not be handed over to the planting Colonists of the opposite coast of Australia. I do hope that Her Majesty's Government will yet show some firmness regarding New Guinea—"indignation meetings" at places in Northern Queensland, Cooktown and the rest, notwithstanding.

Then, after what we are told of the predominance of plutocrats and speculators in New Zealand, and their failure so to manage their own magnificent country as to lead to its sufficient agricultural development by real farmers, would it be just or reasonable to make over to them the Fiji natives hitherto protected by a paternal Government, or to let them possess themselves of the comparatively civilised Samoan and Tongan groups?

In South Africa again the Cape Colony seems to have enough to do in managing its own affairs and its great territory. The large proportion of natives within the Colony proper seems to be about as much as the Colonists can safely deal with; throwing in large native populations beyond those limits seriously disturbs the balance. Their management of outlying native territories has not been by any means successful. The practice of our conquering and making over to them many such territories; letting them keep those which they think more or less profitable, so long as they are profitable, and hand them back to us when they seem troublesome and unprofitable, seems a very objectionable one. Apart from the question of making the Cape Colony and the Boer Republics responsible for their own relations with the interior of Africa, which I now reserve, I think that the most of the native territories already subjected or brought under control by us, should be retained by us. It so happens that from the Kei River border all the way to the Portuguese frontier at Delagoa Bay, there is a territory practically native, easily accessible to us from the sea, and cut off from the rest of Africa by self-governing or foreign possessions. It comprises the Transkei territory, Pondoland and Basutoland, Natal (in which the natives are more than ten to one), Zululand and the Swazis and Amatongas, so far as we may have relations with them—not so very large a territory after all. I have long thought that we might well combine all these into one organised dominion under the Crown, consisting partly of British territory, and partly of protected Native States. After all, the handful of whites in Natal whose representatives are always passing resolutions proposing to take upon themselves the government of territories extended to any extent (with the support, I presume, of British troops), are not more important than the European settlers in several parts of India. Everything cannot be conceded to their desire for domination and speculation.

I am very much an economist, but, after all, we are not so poor that we cannot afford to do our duty by people whose administration we have undertaken. If we would but save the millions we are continually spending on unnecessary and injurious wars, or preparations for war, we could afford to spend thousands to keep up a proper Commission for the Pacific and New Guinea, and find a decent government for a corner of South-East Africa.

The general question of the best mode of administering the Crown Colonies and other territories is a very difficult one—it is much easier to see and point out the defects of our present want of system than to find the remedy—and a solution can hardly be suggested till we settle several previous questions which I have left open when previously touching on them. We want to settle first our home affairs, so that our Parliament and Government may be tolerably efficient, and it may be possible to establish an efficient administration at home for the conduct of Imperial affairs, so far as they must be controlled and regulated there. Then we must make up our minds whether we are really prepared to maintain a considerable Colonial dominion in addition to an Indian dominion; and especially whether we accept and will adhere to the duty of protecting the natives to whom we have promised protection. Where those natives are so sparse and so little fecund, and so little fitted for rough labour that more population is required to cultivate and develop the country, we must settle from what sources that population is to be derived, on what terms and conditions, and how we are to reconcile the respective claims of natives, new settlers, and white enterprisers.

Supposing these questions to be settled, the general principle to which I incline is, that half-and-half systems do not succeed—that you must either have real self-government or a paternal government. Where there are large native or coloured populations, I wholly distrust self-government in the hands of planters, and much misdoubt government by modern speculative and commercial Joint Stock companies, the memory of the East India Company notwithstanding. I think that in all these cases, either you must really and truly give the coloured people a large share of representation in any elective system, or if that cannot be, you must come to paternal government after all. In the latter case I would fashion the government of tropical and other territories mainly populated by coloured people, on the model of our Indian administration in the main—administering British territories with an equal hand for the benefit of all, and protecting and preserving native rule wherever we find it under conditions in which it is just and politic to maintain it. For instance, if New Guinea turns out in any degree to correspond to the descriptions which I have quoted, I would rigorously confine our self-assumed functions to the protection of the natives from external aggression, would not allow European settlement and enterprise to be carried on in a manner which might conflict with native laws, institutions, and ideas, and would uphold the right of the people of New Guinea to New Guinea.

It may well be that in some of the islands of the Pacific and elsewhere the people are so savage, so given to internecine war, and so exposed to aggression, that, as in so much of India, it really may be right and beneficial to assume direct rule over them; but it should be done in such a way that their complete protection should be secured.

As in India so in these territories I would encourage and develop all the local self-government that is possible without bringing about a conflict of races or injustice to the weaker race. And as in India I would look to the possibility of a future day when institutions might be so developed, and conflicting interests and ideas so far reconciled, that a larger self-government might be introduced, in which white, black, and brown might partake on equal terms, and by means of which we might be in great part relieved of a continually increasing task, growing too heavy for us. But in most of the territories, where the population is mixed, and the European settlers are still divided by broad lines from the people, that day has not yet come.

I may add that we must also exercise some restraint on the liberty of British subjects to go where they like and to call on their Government to follow and protect them. If they thus go into countries already occupied by natives, they must either do so at their own risk, or submit to such limitations and control as the Government may find it necessary to impose.

CHAPTER XI.

AFRICA.

AFRICA, in the widest sense, has been left out of the above view, and I now come to it. It is a very large exception indeed from the statement that there are no more worlds to conquer. To realise how large Africa is, compare it with India on the map, and see how many Indias could be put into it. Deserts there, no doubt, are, but most of it seems to be a sufficiently watered and habitable country, and though we know little of its resources, we can at least say, in general terms, that very much of it is fertile, and capable of supporting large populations.

First as to our own position in Africa. We have seen how we stand in South Africa. The self-governing Cape Colony proper, excluding the unrepresented Transkei, has an area about the size of France. There are no very recent statistics of population, but the whites (English and Dutch together) seem to be nearly 300,000; the coloured people about 600,000—total under a million. All the other territories, from the Kei to Delagoa Bay, may be roughly put at little more than half the size of the Cape Colony, with a population of from a million to a million and a half, of whom the whites are certainly not 5 per cent. Bechuanaland, as annexed or formally protected, is again about the size of France, or rather more, with a population very small indeed in proportion to its size, probably under 200,000 in all. The Orange Free State, with an area about the size of England, numbers only about 140,000, of whom one-half are whites. It is the policy there not to allow a

L

preponderance of blacks. The Transvaal territory is about the size of the United Kingdom, and is estimated to have about 750,000 inhabitants, of whom only about 40,000 or 50,000 are whites, and the rest are Africans in a very indigenous state, many of them rather tributary tribes than proper subjects.

Though Bechuanaland is little fertile and very little populated, we have on that side the way opened to us to the interior of Africa, and to countries larger and, in some degree, better populated in that direction. There is, however, in some sense, a limit to that. The country to the west we have conceded to Germany, from the Cape boundary to that of the Portuguese on the west coast. On the east we are shut off by the Transvaal and the Eastern Portuguese territories. And in the regions to the north any idea of trade to Cape Town could hardly be carried much beyond the Zambesi; beyond that the outlets are evidently to the east and the west. Farther north, too, we come to the watershed of the Congo, consecrated by anticipation to a general international trade. That arrangement seems to extend almost right across the continent. And again the countries about Zanzibar, not possessed by the Sultan of that place, seem to have been pretty well surrendered as a field for German exploration and annexation, so far as the Germans choose to occupy them. South Africa might in general terms be defined as the part of that continent south of about 15° South Latitude; and in all the interior part between our present frontier and that point, there is, no doubt, room for much extension if we wish for it.

It has been said we know little of the claims of the African Company on the Niger, and that the British Colonies, north of that river, are scattered, and have not yet large dominions. On the east, the last partition with Germany seems to have left us a considerable field, but we have not yet availed ourselves of it. For the rest, if Zanzibar (though the island has many British subjects from India) is not in any degree under our protection, and Perim and Socotra are not counted African, we have nothing till we come to Suakim on the Red Sea. That place, though nominally Egyptian, is managed by us, and practically garrisoned by us; for, though happily we have been able to substitute Egyptian for British soldiers, we pay for them. So it is to be presumed that if any interests are subserved by holding Suakim, now that the Soudan is definitively abandoned, they are our interests. But what those interests are no man can explain. If there is any idea of an interest somewhere, it seems to be that after having slaughtered very many of the tribes, we may, by wearing and worrying them, at length make them friendly, and induce them to trade with us when they have nothing left to trade. At any rate, we seem to have been carrying on a little war, blockading the coast, subsidising one set of tribes to fight against another set, and exulting greatly when the so-called friends (that is, those who take our money and our arms) gain any advantage over the other set. There is something very sad in the way in which the Soudan country, so long comparatively peaceful and subject to civilising influences of a sort, and the great waterways of the Upper Nile, have now been given over to anarchy and desolation; but at all events, if we no longer desire to establish ourselves there, we might leave the people alone, and not continue hostility and enmities. That seems to be the view taken by our own best officers. It is to be gathered from the last Egyptian Blue Book that they, too, are themselves ignorant of the objects which we have in view. We are told that if we wish to keep Suakim and remain on the defensive, that place is quite impregnable to any attack which the natives are capable of making; also that the maritime blockade, however stringent, can have little effect on the real situation in the Soudan. The present

Governor, Watson Pasha, very sensibly says (Memo of April 6, 1886)—"If the Government were to declare that the war was at an end, and to re-open trade, it is possible that after a time the country would settle down."

Besides the German claims already mentioned, they have a settlement at the Cameroons, south of the Niger mouth. The Portuguese claim long stretches of the coast countries south of the equator, on both east and west coasts; and the French claim a large territory on one side of the Congo mouth. The French and other countries have Colonies of sorts alternating with ours on the west coast north of the equator. The French and Italians have the ports of Obok, Assab, and Massowah on the east coast adjoining Abyssinia. We know that the French hold North Africa, except Egypt and Tripoli (the last mostly desert) and the dominions of the Sultan of Morocco.

For the rest, the whole vast interior, except so far as it is appropriated by the international Congo State, and including the Soudan and equatorial regions once under Egypt, are now, so far as European and civilised Powers are concerned, a no man's land, of only parts of which do we know anything, and of little of which do we know much. This much, however, we do know, from our connection with Egypt and the enterprise of our explorers in the region of the great lakes, that a large part of Africa in that direction is elevated and fertile, and apparently might be suitable for European enterprise and industry. The Moka coffee (the name under which that article first became well known in Europe) is understood to have come from this part of Africa.

Of other parts of Africa we have glimpses sufficient to induce us to believe that there are populous countries, with some degree of organised government, especially those in the northern half of the continent, to which the Mahommedan religion and some Mahommedan civilisation have in some degree penetrated.

But it may be said in general terms that over a very large proportion of the continent so much anarchy, inter-slaving wars, desolation, and misery prevail, that the intervention of any European Power capable of introducing peace, order, and material comfort would be at least as justifiable as our intervention in India.

The people, too, have much capacity for labour and many virtues. We know enough of them in the shape of the mixture of many African races who were the slaves of America, and are now freemen there, to say that they make good Christians and very tolerable citizens when, in spite of generations of the worst kind of slavery, they have at last a chance. Some of those who have come under civilising influences in our own African Colonies also exhibit many good qualities. If they have not the native intelligence and civilisation of the people of India, they have greater physical robustness.

I have often thought that, if we had not India on our hands, we might have taken advantage of the opportunities we have had, both in the north and in the south of the African Continent, to establish a great empire there; but, with India and so many other possessions to hold, it may not be—to say nothing of the jealousies of Foreign Powers if we attempt to take everything. The resources in men of our limited islands are already sufficiently strained to supply an army adequate both for home security and for the great garrisons abroad. Whatever opinion may be as to the practicability of moderate extensions, I think it must be generally felt that we could not undertake another large empire. Tempting, then, as, in some respects, Africa may be, we must be cautious and not allow ourselves to be carried too far there, or to drift into complications involving greater advances than we are prepared for. No; we must limit ourselves in Africa.

In South Africa we must, I think, draw a line beyond

which we will not go. The way to the interior from the north of Africa we have already surrendered, for we shall hardly march forward from Suakim again. We must warn the African Company on the west not to attempt too much, and look after them if their territorialism turns out to be serious. We must not yield to the seductions of local merchants and Chambers of Commerce in this country seeking to establish large dominions in North-western Africa. As regards South Africa, what we have to do is to make up our minds about Bechuanaland. It is undoubtedly very difficult to draw an artificial line at the twenty-second parallel with no natural boundary. We must either compensate Makroane and Montisoia, come away, and let the Boers have their will after all; or we must make up our minds to hold the country, pay for its administration, and risk inevitable extensions; or we must still try to bribe or coax the Cape Colony to take it off our hands, and either hold it, or come to some confederative arrangement with the Boer Republics for holding the interior of South Africa. In the latter case we could not again interfere between them and the natives. It is certainly a very puzzling situation. The worst of it is that, if the Cape Colony did take Bechuanaland, they might afterwards come to grief and cast it back upon us, so that the last state would be worse than the first. If the trade route, which was the principal justification for the advance, is at all a reality, that is entirely for the benefit of the Cape Colony. I think we may at least put our foot down and say we will have none of it unless there is some fair arrangement with the Colony regarding transit from the coast and Customs duties. To tell the truth, if we have not the courage to come away and allow the Cape Colony and the Boer Republics to do as they like in South Africa, and confederate if they can, I fear that the Bechuana expedition and the acts following on it have committed us to a large dominion in the interior of South Africa, which must probably in the end extend to the Zambesi or thereabouts. But, even if that must be, I hope we may come at length to some frontier where we may stop and avoid an ever-extending dominion, which might become an empire. No doubt a confederation of the Cape Colony and the Boer Republics would probably be strong enough to hold their own in those countries; but if we accept that arrangement, we must be quite clear that we are not to interfere again. And perhaps it might in that case be difficult to maintain our hold over South Africa as really a British dominion.

If we do not desire to establish in Africa any more extensive empire than we can help, and are content with what we have got there or cannot avoid, we need not be jealous of foreign nations who may wish to take what we do not want, but might rather encourage them to expend their energies in Africa wherever they can fairly and legitimately do so in a manner calculated to advance the interests of mankind.

The great Congo basin has been (it has been said), by international agreement, consecrated to the common commerce of all, and cannot be exclusively occupied by particular Powers for their own benefit. The Congo State (so called—a very little *in esse* and very much *in posse*) is to be a sort of international guardian of this agreement, and is precluded from exercising territorial jurisdiction in such a way as to conflict with the general right to free-trade in those regions. The benevolent motives and great liberality of the King of the Belgians, as personally the principal promoter of this neutral State, are beyond doubt. And if it goes on, we may very heartily wish it well. We may well hope, too, for the success of the projects for railways to connect the lower Congo with the navigable upper rivers, and for flotillas to navigate that upper river, which are in hand.

The Germans have got rather into an *impasse* on the south-western coast, between the desert and the deep sea. They will not make much of what we have conceded to them there, and it is perhaps as well that they are not very seriously settled so near us in South Africa. But farther north, whether on the east, or west by the Cameroons, if they like to push their possessions we need not object. If they will fairly and honestly undertake African rule and not leave it too exclusively to commercial companies, they may be a great civilising influence.

The Italians are a clever people, with some surplus population, considerable resources, no Colonies, and a turn towards Africa. They have a small place called Assab, and have most patiently endured their lot in being presented with that miserable share of African extension—Massowah, where they come into collision with the Abyssinians. Why should we not offer them Suakim and our share of the east coast as now settled with the Germans? They might then seriously think of obtaining an entrance to the upper Nile, the Victoria Nyanza, and the interior of tropical Africa, and might be more successful than we have been in coming to terms with the Arabs. It would be a good thing that they should share with us anxiety to protect the Suez Canal. And if they succeeded on the upper Nile, that would go far to cover Egypt. Not impossibly they might come to terms with the French so far as to get rid of the small French settlements in that quarter, which we should be very glad of.

On the other hand, the question of Egypt apart, I do not know why we should be jealous of any French extensions in the north and north-west of Africa. The French would be better and perhaps more legitimately occupied there than in some other parts of the world.

If we could get rid of that excessive jealousy of any other Power doing what we do so often and so much, I do think that, holding our own in South Africa and in such other African possessions as are worth keeping, we might very well leave the rest to others.

Egypt is quite another matter. Of that I shall say but little. I quite believe that if we were in Egypt with the goodwill of other nations, and could stay there and administer it as we administer India, and if we could begin without an overwhelming debt, we might in that case make a very good job of a rich country and a good people. But it is far otherwise. We are in Egypt under circumstances of great disadvantage, and we are solemnly bound neither to stay there permanently nor to turn our occupation to our own selfish advantage. Practically we only hold our present position there on condition of paying the interest of the debt, which we cannot do without great sacrifices on our part. While the revenue goes to pay the bondholders, we defend Egypt, and the British taxpayer pays for that defence. Our administration is so hampered by foreign privileges and other conditions, which foreign Powers, jealous of our position there, will not relax, that it cannot be rendered satisfactory.

I have always maintained that to say that we will stay till we establish a good and a stable government, capable of meeting all its obligations, is in effect saying that we will stay till the Greek Kalends. We might possibly establish a government which might administer the country in a tolerable way, judged by an Oriental standard, and which, after a revolution or two, might settle down ; but a native government which shall both satisfy the people of Egypt and, at the same time, satisfy the foreign bondholders, is quite impossible. To say nothing of other difficulties, none of the recent budget schemes make any adequate provision whatever for the defensive armaments so necessary as Egypt is situated.

We must look the debt question in the face, for, say what

we will of philanthropy and good government, that is the crucial question. We talk as if we had improved the financial position; we have done nothing of the kind. What we have done is to stop the sinking funds, and so save a large outgoing; but, by doing so, we have deprived the people of all prospect of ultimate relief. Meantime we have piled debt upon debt; the last guaranteed nine millions is a clear addition to the debt in a pre-preference form. In addition to all that, the change in the value of gold has enhanced the whole debt, diminished the value of the produce from which it is paid, and made the taxes a heavier burden on the people.

When Lord Salisbury says once more that we are not to leave Egypt till our mission is fulfilled, I cannot help thinking that he puts us in the position of the man who has rashly undertaken the hopelessly embarrassed estate of an incapable young friend, very much against the will of the other relations, and vows he will never give it up till he has cured all the faults of the owner, and has insured a thoroughly satisfactory management, and complete solvency. He finds that the young man is not to be taught; that he can only attain such tolerable management as paid agents can achieve in spite of every drawback and every opposition from the other relations; and that solvency is farther off than ever. To keep the thing going at all, the guardian is obliged not only to sacrifice much labour, time, trouble, and temper, but to expend very much from his own pocket on ruinous litigations and the defence of the estate, without in any degree gaining his end or contenting the people on the estate. It may be that having once got the management he may obstinately insist on keeping it till things are righted; and that as things never do come right, that gives him an indefinite tenure. But since he gains nothing and loses much by the position, why should he wish to continue it? That seems to me to be our position in Egypt. I should say that our tenure of that country is so embarrassing, costly, and unsatisfactory, that we should be only too desirous to get out of it. We should need no urging; the only question for us should be—how we can get out of it.

CHAPTER XII.

CONCLUSION.

AND now to conclude. We certainly have a magnificent Empire which may well satisfy us, and an ample outlet for our people of all classes. We need not grumble that our Empire has pretty well reached the limits set by Nature, and that we cannot continue to go forward so fast as in the last few years. We may be well content to improve and fill up what we have; there is still in that a great task before us, which will give us ample scope for a long time to come, and we need not restlessly ask for more. We may hope that if things go on as they are, with a few necessary adjustments, we may continue to be on the nearest terms of friendly alliance with our greater Colonies, even when they have grown into peoples so considerable that they may hardly occupy the position of children; while in India and the Crown Colonies, for which we are more directly responsible, the great thing is to try to do our duty by the people, to make them prosperous and contented, and to prepare them for a greater or less amount of self-management, as far as is possible, rather than permit ourselves to be too nervously anxious lest some day some one should want to take them from us. Perhaps some day we may cede our Protectorates or possessions in the Pacific to a great Australian Federation which has occupied its own territories, and has grown up to a full measure of parental capacity; but that is not yet, nor for some time to come.

Whatever may be our arrangements for the government of African territories, I contemplate retaining a strong British hold on the southern and south-eastern end of that

Continent, and look on the route of which that is the halfway house as our true route to India in time of difficulty and danger. The northern route, by the Mediterranean and the Red Sea, I look on as a mercantile and a peace route. I greatly doubt and distrust the possibility, the expediency, and the paying-ness of attempting to maintain and cover that great length of voyage through land-locked seas in case of war with a great Mediterranean Power, and have little trust in the efficiency of the so-called chain of fortresses, with many hundred miles between each link. We should not only have fully to garrison and maintain those posts, but to guard with a superior naval force all the seas between them, besides keeping a large army in Egypt, if we are to hold that link, too, by force. I am very much convinced that even if we could maintain that route in time of war, it would cost us infinitely more than it is worth; that it would be infinitely cheaper to use the Cape route; and that even in point of time, the ten days (or, at the very most, a fortnight) gained in time of peace by the Mediterranean route, would be more than lost by the delays inevitable to convoys and precautions in time of war.

I confess that, if I had my way, I should like to withdraw our Mediterranean fleet and add it to the Channel fleet, so as to make us thoroughly secure in that vital quarter; and that we should then appear in the Mediterranean only as merchants and owners of transports. Leaving the politics of the Mediterranean and the Bosphorus for the most part to the Powers and peoples of the Mediterranean and their immediate allies, I would have it that we should take part only in respect of our share in the comity of European nations, and as interested in Eastern Europe in a very secondary degree. In a much greater degree we should be interested in that internationalisation of the Suez Canal for peaceful purposes to which recent engagements tend, and to which sound policy points. If we could not use it in the unhappy event of serious war, we might, at least, when occasion may require, put forth our naval strength to block it, and prevent its being used against us by any one else. As regards international arrangements for the canal in peace, I believe the quarantine question is the only one likely to give much trouble—foreigners are so sensitive about that, and it touches us so nearly.

Public opinion is probably not yet ripe for giving up our military posts in the Mediterranean, or turning them into mere coaling stations; but it is becoming more and more evident to all what a serious difficulty and embarrassment our position in Egypt is, and how much it embitters our relations with other Powers, especially with France. Possibly there is more smoke than fire in the outcry of the French press, for behind the French press there is another power in France, the Bourse, and that power we are bribing by paying the bondholders their full coupons. The French public is an investing public, and the price of the Funds influences them as much as national sentiment, even in its tenderest places. But, meantime, the British taxpayer is paying for the army which guards and defends Egypt, a function which must always be performed by some army costing much money.

After all, why should we be involved in all these difficulties on account of the Egyptian bondholders? Why should they of all foreign bondholders be the only creditors whose debts are to be enforced by foreign armies, any more than Turkish, or Spanish, or South American bondholders? The French bondholders are, no doubt, a strong power; but the French sentiment against our holding Egypt is also much excited. If really and truly our only object is to insure the freedom of the Suez Canal, and not to secure the bondholders, surely we had better try to make some arrangement by which the former object may be effected.

The French Government have repeatedly offered an

engagement that if we leave Egypt they will not go there. Why not take advantage of this proposal and try to make an international self-denying treaty regarding Egypt, even if some sacrifice of the bondholders is involved, and they must take their chance of getting from a native Government what the country can fairly pay, like other foreign bondholders? That seems to be the only hope of getting out of Egypt in a satisfactory way. If no such arrangement is made, then, no doubt, as soon as we come out, the foreign bondholders will seek to re-enter in some other way. We are in a terrible difficulty. To stay is a very severe drain on our army and finance, and ruinous to good-will between ourselves and our European neighbours; to go away is very difficult. Why did we ever go when the French wished to stay away? There is no doubt that Egypt is the skeleton at our national feast.

Undoubtedly it would be a great relief to us if Egypt could be almost independent, as in fact it was from the time of Mehemet Ali to that of Ismael. And it would greatly tend to our peace of mind if we could concern ourselves less in the politics of Western Asia. We are apt to excite ourselves unnecessarily. At one time we are keen for the necessity of maintaining the Turkish Empire, and accept the ridiculous fiction, of modern invention, that the Indian Mahommedans reverence the Grand Turk as Caliph At another time we are persuaded of the danger of a Ma hommedan revival, which is once more to threaten Christendom. Thinking as I do, that there is a very great amount of good in the Mahommedan religion, and that, Turks, Arabs, Persians, and some other Mahommedans are very fine races with great capabilities, I do not deny that, if it were possible, it would be very desirable to have a great Mahommedan State or federation in Western Asia. Such a Power would have a very steadying and conservative effect. But I fear nothing of the kind is possible. The Ottoman Turks are, no doubt, a particularly fine race, but all told they are not an exceedingly numerous people; their government is execrable, and effete beyond recovery. Now that they are in decadence the Arab hatred and contempt for them has broken out. Where then is there any possibility of any large Mahommedan union? On the contrary, the various Mahommedan races are antagonistic in the last degree. Arabs hate Turks, Persians and Kurds hate equally Turks and Arabs. There is a bitter antagonism between Affghans and Persians on the one side, and Affghans and Turkomans on the other. The only common bond of all might be a common hatred of invading foreigners. And our best security against any combination hostile to us is the difficulty which others must experience in dealing with these peoples, and the antagonism sure to be created by attempts to bring them under control. We had much better be content to regard India as a self-contained possession to which we have always free access by the ocean route, and not vex ourselves too greatly over the politics of the rest of Asia.

If we take a general view of the British Empire, we shall see that, notwithstanding the variety and spread of our great Empire, by far the greatest part of our population, strength, and resources are concentrated in the British Islands and India. Thus:—

	Population.
British Isles...	Thirty-six millions.
India	Two hundred and fifty millions, over whom we have complete control.
White Colonies	Eight millions, over most of whom we have no control.
Colonies, etc., mainly inhabited by coloured races	Nine millions, over whom we exercise an imperfect control.

Selections from Cassell & Company's Publications.

Illustrated, Fine-Art, and other Volumes.

Art, The Magazine of. Yearly Vol. With 500 choice Engravings. 16s.
After London; or, **Wild England.** By RICHARD JEFFERIES. 3s. 6d.
Along Alaska's Great River. By F. SCHWATKA. Illustrated. 12s. 6d.
Appreciation of Gold. 6d.
Artist, Education of the. By E. CHESNEAU. Translated by CLARA BELL. 5s.
Behind Time. By GEORGE PARSONS LATHROP. Illustrated. 2s. 6d.
Bimetallism, The Theory of. By D. BARBOUR. 6s.
Bismarck, Prince. By CHARLES LOWE, M.A. Two Vols. 24s.
Bright, John, Life and Times of. By W. ROBERTSON. 7s. 6d.
British Ballads. With 275 Original Illustrations. Two Vols. 7s. 6d. each.
British Battles on Land and Sea. By JAMES GRANT. With about 600 Illustrations. Three Vols., 4to, £1 7s.; Library Edition, £1 10s.
British Battles, Recent. Illustrated. 4to, 9s.; Library Edition, 10s.
Browning, An Introduction to the Study of. By A. SYMONS. 2s. 6d.
British Empire, The. By Sir GEORGE CAMPBELL, M.P. 3s.
Butterflies and Moths, European. By W. F. KIRBY. With 61 Coloured Plates. Demy 4to, 35s.
Canaries and Cage-Birds, The Illustrated Book of. By W. A. BLAKSTON, W. SWAYSLAND, and A. F. WIENER. With 56 Fac-simile Coloured Plates, 35s. Half-morocco, £2 5s.
Cannibals and Convicts. By JULIAN THOMAS ("The Vagabond"). 10s. 6d.
Cassell's Family Magazine. Yearly Vol. Illustrated. 9s.
Cathedral Churches of England and Wales. Illustrated. 21s.
Celebrities of the Century: being a Dictionary of Men and Women of the Nineteenth Century. 21s.; Roxburgh, 25s.
Chess Problem, The. A Text-Book, with Illustrations. 7s. 6d.
Children of the Cold, The. By Lieut. SCHWATKA. 2s. 6d.
Choice Poems by H. W. Longfellow. Illustrated from Paintings by his Son, ERNEST W. LONGFELLOW. Small 4to, cloth, 6s.
Choice Dishes at Small Cost. By A. G. PAYNE. 1s.
Christmas in the Olden Time. By Sir WALTER SCOTT, with charming Original Illustrations. 7s. 6d.
Cities of the World: their Origin, Progress, and Present Aspect. Three Vols. Illustrated. 7s. 6d. each.
Civil Service, Guide to Employment in the. 3s. 6d.
Civil Service.—Guide to Female Employment in Government Offices. 1s.
Clinical Manuals for Practitioners and Students of Medicine. A List of Volumes forwarded post free on application to the Publishers.
Clothing, The Influence of, on Health. By F. TREVES, F.R.C.S. 2s.
Colonies and India, Our, How we Got Them, and Why we Keep Them. By Prof. C. RANSOME. 1s.
Columbus, Christopher, The Life and Voyages of. By WASHINGTON IRVING. Three Vols. 7s. 6d.
Cookery, Cassell's Dictionary of. Containing about Nine Thousand Recipes. 7s. 6d.; Roxburgh, 10s. 6d.
Co-operators, Working Men: What they have Done, and What they are Doing. By A. H. DYKE-ACLAND, M.P., and B. JONES. 1s.
Cookery, A Year's. By PHYLLIS BROWNE. 3s. 6d.
Cook Book, Catherine Owen's New. 4s.
Countries of the World, The. By ROBERT BROWN, M.A., Ph.D., &c. Complete in Six Vols., with about 750 Illustrations. 4to, 7s. 6d. each.
Cromwell, Oliver: The Man and his Mission. By J. ALLANSON PICTON, M.P. Cloth, 7s. 6d.; morocco, cloth sides, 9s.
Cyclopædia, Cassell's Concise. With 12,000 subjects, brought down to the latest date. With about 600 Illustrations. 15s.; Roxburgh, 18s.

5 G. 2.87

Selections from Cassell & Company's Publications.

Dairy Farming. By Prof. J. P. SHELDON. With 25 Fac-simile Coloured Plates, and numerous Wood Engravings. Cloth, 31s. 6d.; half-morocco, 42s.

Decisive Events in History. By THOMAS ARCHER. With Sixteen Illustrations. Boards, 3s. 6d.; cloth, 5s.

Decorative Design. By CHRISTOPHER DRESSER, Ph.D. Illustrated. 5s.

Deserted Village Series, The. Consisting of *Éditions de luxe* of the most favourite poems of Standard Authors. Illustrated. 2s. 6d. each.

SONGS FROM SHAKESPEARE. MILTON'S L'ALLEGRO AND IL PENSEROSO.	GOLDSMITH'S DESERTED VILLAGE. WORDSWORTH'S ODE ON IMMORTALITY, AND LINES ON TINTERN ABBEY.

Dickens, Character Sketches from. SECOND and THIRD SERIES. With Six Original Drawings in each by F. BARNARD. In Portfolio, 21s. each.

Diary of Two Parliaments. By W. H. LUCY. Vol. I.: The Disraeli Parliament. Vol. II.: The Gladstone Parliament. 12s. each.

Dog, The. By IDSTONE. Illustrated. 2s. 6d.

Dog, Illustrated Book of the. By VERO SHAW, B.A. With 28 Coloured Plates. Cloth bevelled, 35s.; half-morocco, 45s.

Domestic Dictionary, The. Cloth, 7s. 6d.

Doré's Adventures of Munchausen. Illustrated by GUSTAVE DORÉ. 5s.

Doré's Dante's Inferno. Illustrated by GUSTAVE DORÉ. 21s.

Doré's Fairy Tales Told Again. With Engravings by DORÉ. 5s.

Doré Gallery, The. With 250 Illustrations by DORÉ. 4to, 42s.

Doré's Milton's Paradise Lost. Illustrated by DORÉ. 4to, 21s.

Edinburgh, Old and New. Three Vols. With 600 Illustrations. 9s. each.

Egypt: Descriptive, Historical, and Picturesque. By Prof. G. EBERS. Translated by CLARA BELL, with Notes by SAMUEL BIRCH, LL.D., &c. Two Vols. With 800 Original Engravings. Vol. I., £2 5s.; Vol. II., £2 12s. 6d. Complete in box, £4 17s. 6d.

Electricity in the Service of Man. With nearly 850 Illustrations. 21s.

Electricity, Practical. By Prof. W. E. AYRTON. 7s. 6d.

Electricity, Age of, from Amber Soul to Telephone. By PARK BENJAMIN, Ph.D. 7s. 6d.

Electrician's Pocket-Book, The. By GORDON WIGAN, M.A. 5s.

Encyclopædic Dictionary, The. A New and Original Work of Reference to all the Words in the English Language. Eleven Divisional Vols. now ready, 10s. 6d. each; or the Double Divisional Vols., half-morocco, 21s. each.

Energy in Nature. By WM. LANT CARPENTER, B.A., B.Sc. 80 Illustrations. 3s. 6d.

England, Cassell's Illustrated History of. With 2,000 Illustrations. Ten Vols., 4to, 9s. each.

English History, The Dictionary of. Cloth, 21s.; Roxburgh, 25s.

English Literature, Library of. By Prof. HENRY MORLEY. Five Vols., 7s. 6d. each.

    VOL. I.—SHORTER ENGLISH POEMS.
    VOL. II.—ILLUSTRATIONS OF ENGLISH RELIGION.
    VOL. III.—ENGLISH PLAYS.
    VOL. IV.—SHORTER WORKS IN ENGLISH PROSE.
    VOL. V.—SKETCHES OF LONGER WORKS IN ENGLISH VERSE AND PROSE.

Five Volumes handsomely bound in half-morocco, £5 5s.

English Literature, The Story of. By ANNA BUCKLAND. 3s. 6d.

English Literature, Morley's First Sketch of. *Revised Edition,* 7s. 6d.

Selections from Cassell & Company's Publications.

English Literature, Dictionary of. By W. DAVENPORT ADAMS. *Cheap Edition*, 7s. 6d.; Roxburgh, 10s. 6d.
English Poetesses. By ERIC S. ROBERTSON, M.A. 5s.
English Writers. By Prof. HENRY MORLEY. Vol. I. Crown 8vo, cloth, 5s.
Etching. By S. K. KOEHLER. With 30 Full-Page Plates by Old and Modern Etchers. £4 4s.
Etiquette of Good Society. 1s.; cloth, 1s. 6d.
Exceptional Distress. 6d.
Eye, Ear, and Throat, The Management of the. 3s. 6d.
False Hopes. By Prof. GOLDWIN SMITH, M.A., LL.D., D.C.L. 6d.
Family Physician, The. By Eminent PHYSICIANS and SURGEONS. Cloth, 21s.; half-morocco, 25s.
Fenn, G. Manville, Works by. Cloth boards, 2s. each

SWEET MACE.	THE VICAR'S PEOPLE.
DUTCH THE DIVER.	COBWEB'S FATHER.
MY PATIENTS. Being the Notes of a Navy Surgeon.	THE PARSON O' DUMFORD. POVERTY CORNER.

Ferns, European. By JAMES BRITTEN, F.L.S. With 30 Fac-simile Coloured Plates by D. BLAIR, F.L.S. 21s.
Field Naturalist's Handbook, The. By the Rev. J. G. WOOD and THEODORE WOOD. 5s.
Figuier's Popular Scientific Works. With Several Hundred Illustrations in each. 3s. 6d. each.

THE HUMAN RACE.	THE OCEAN WORLD.
WORLD BEFORE THE DELUGE.	THE VEGETABLE WORLD.
REPTILES AND BIRDS.	THE INSECT WORLD.
MAMMALIA.	

Fine-Art Library, The. Edited by JOHN SPARKES, Principal of the South Kensington Art Schools. Each Book contains about 100 Illustrations. 5s. each.

ENGRAVING. By Le Vicomte Henri Delaborde. Translated by R. A. M. Stevenson.	THE EDUCATION OF THE ARTIST. By Ernest Chesneau. Translated by Clara Bell. (Not illustrated.)
TAPESTRY. By Eugène Müntz. Translated by Miss L. J. Davis.	GREEK ARCHÆOLOGY. By Maxime Collignon. Translated by Dr. J. H. Wright.
THE ENGLISH SCHOOL OF PAINTING. By E. Chesneau. Translated by L. N. Etherington. With an Introduction by Prof. Ruskin.	ARTISTIC ANATOMY. By Prof. Duval. Translated by F. E. Fenton.
THE FLEMISH SCHOOL OF PAINTING. By A. J. Wauters. Translated by Mrs. Henry Rossel.	THE DUTCH SCHOOL OF PAINTING. By Henry Havard. Translated by G. Powell.

Fisheries of the World, The. Illustrated. 4to. 9s.
Five Pound Note, The, and other Stories. By G. S. JEALOUS. 1s.
Flowers, and How to Paint Them. By MAUD NAFTEL. With Coloured Plates. 5s.
Forging of the Anchor, The. A Poem. By Sir SAMUEL FERGUSON, LL.D. With 20 Original Illustrations. Gilt edges, 5s.
Fossil Reptiles, A History of British. By Sir RICHARD OWEN, K.C.B., F.R.S., &c. With 268 Plates. In Four Vols., £12 12s.
Four Years of Irish History (1845-49). By Sir GAVAN DUFFY, K.C.M.G. 21s.
Franco-German War, Cassell's History of the. Two Vols. With 500 Illustrations. 9s. each.
Fresh-water Fishes of Europe, The. By Prof. H. G. SEELEY, F.R.S. Cloth, 21s.

Selections from Cassell & Company's Publications.

From Gold to Grey. Being Poems and Pictures of Life and Nature. By MARY D. BRINE. Illustrated. 7s. 6d.
Garden Flowers, Familiar. By SHIRLEY HIBBERD. With Coloured Plates by F. E. HULME, F.L.S. Complete in Five Series. 12s. 6d. each.
Gardening, Cassell's Popular. Illustrated. 4 vols., 5s. each.
Geometrical Drawing for Army Candidates. By H. T. LILLEY, M.A. 2s.
Geometry, Practical Solid. By MAJOR ROSS. 2s.
Gladstone, Life of W. E. By G. BARNETT SMITH. With Portrait, 3s. 6d. *Jubilee Edition*, 1s.
Gleanings from Popular Authors. Two Vols. With Original Illustrations. 4to, 9s. each. Two Vols. in One, 15s.
Great Industries of Great Britain. Three Vols. With about 400 Illustrations. 4to, cloth, 7s. 6d. each.
Great Painters of Christendom, The, from Cimabue to Wilkie. By JOHN FORBES-ROBERTSON. Illustrated throughout. 12s. 6d.
Great Northern Railway, The Official Illustrated Guide to the. 1s.; or in cloth, 2s.
Great Western Railway, The Official Illustrated Guide to the. *New and Revised Edition.* With Illustrations, 1s.; cloth, 2s.
Gulliver's Travels. With 88 Engravings by MORTEN. *Cheap Edition.* Cloth, 3s. 6d.; cloth gilt, 5s.
Gun and its Development, The. By W. W. GREENER. With 500 Illustrations. 10s. 6d.
Health, The Book of. By Eminent Physicians and Surgeons. Cloth, 21s.; half-morocco, 25s.
Health, The Influence of Clothing on. By F. TREVES, F.R.G.S. 2s.
Health at School. By CLEMENT DUKES, M.D., B.S. 7s. 6d.
Heavens, The Story of the. By Sir ROBERT STAWELL BALL, F.R.S., F.R.A.S. With Coloured Plates and Wood Engravings. 31s. 6d.
Heroes of Britain in Peace and War. In Two Vols., with 300 Original Illustrations. 5s. each; or One Vol., library binding, 10s. 6d.
Horse Keeper, The Practical. By GEORGE FLEMING, LL.D., F.R.C.V.S. Illustrated. 7s. 6d.
Horse, The Book of the. By SAMUEL SIDNEY With 28 *fac-simile* Coloured Plates. *Enlarged Edition.* Demy 4to, 35s.; half-morocco, 45s.
Horses, The Simple Ailments of. By W. F. Illustrated. 5s.
Household Guide, Cassell's. With Illustrations and Coloured Plates. *New and Cheap Edition*, in Four Vols., 20s.
How Women may Earn a Living. By MERCY GROGAN. 1s.
Imperial White Books. In Quarterly Vols. 10s. 6d. per annum, post free; separately, 3s. 6d. each.
India, The Coming Struggle for. By Prof. VAMBÉRY. 5s.
India, Cassell's History of. By JAMES GRANT. With about 400 Illustrations. Library binding. One Vol. 15s.
India: the Land and the People. By Sir J. CAIRD, K.C.B. 10s. 6d.
Indoor Amusements, Card Games, and Fireside Fun, Cassell's Book of. Illustrated. 3s. 6d.
Invisible Life, Vignettes from. By JOHN BADCOCK, F.R.M.S. Illustrated. 3s. 6d.
Irish Parliament, The; What it Was and What it Did. By J. G. SWIFT MACNEILL, M.A., M.P. 1s.
Italy. By J. W. PROBYN. 7s. 6d.
John Parmelee's Curse. By JULIAN HAWTHORNE. 2s. 6d.
Kennel Guide, The Practical. By Dr. GORDON STABLES. Illustrated. 2s. 6d.
Khiva, A Ride to. By the late Col. FRED. BURNABY. 1s. 6d.
Kidnapped. By R. L. STEVENSON. 5s.
Ladies' Physician, The. A Guide for Women in the Treatment of their Ailments. By a Physician. 6s.

Selections from Cassell & Company's Publications.

Land Question, The. By Prof. J. ELLIOT, M.R.A.C. 10s. 6d.
Landscape Painting in Oils, A Course of Lessons in. By A. F. GRACE. With Nine Reproductions in Colour. *Cheap Edition*, 25s.
Law, About Going to. By A. J. WILLIAMS, M.P. 2s. 6d.
Letts's Diaries and other Time-saving Publications are now published exclusively by CASSELL & COMPANY. (*A list sent post free on application.*)
Liberal, Why I am a. By ANDREW REID. 2s. 6d. *People's Edition.* 1s.
Local Dual Standards. By JOHN HENRY NORMAN. 1s.
London and South Western Railway, The Official Illustrated Guide to the. 1s.; cloth, 2s.
London and North Western Railway, The Official Illustrated Guide to the. 1s.; cloth, 2s.
London, Greater. By EDWARD WALFORD. Two Vols. With about 400 Illustrations. 9s. each.
London, Old and New. Six Vols., each containing about 200 Illustrations and Maps. Cloth, 9s. each.
London's Roll of Fame. With Portraits and Illustrations. 12s. 6d.
Longfellow's Poetical Works. Illustrated throughout, £3 3s.; *Popular Edition*, 16s.
Love's Extremes, At. By MAURICE THOMPSON. 5s.
Martin Luther: His Life and Times. By PETER BAYNE, LL.D. Two Vols., demy 8vo, 1,040 pages. Cloth, 24s.
Mechanics, The Practical Dictionary of. Containing 15,000 Drawings. Four Vols. 21s. each.
Medicine, Manuals for Students of. (*A List forwarded post free.*)
Medical Sciences, International Journal of the. Quarterly Numbers. Each 6s.
Midland Railway, Official Illustrated Guide to the. *New and Revised Edition.* 1s.; cloth, 2s.
Modern Artists, Some. With highly-finished Engravings. 12s. 6d.
Modern Europe, A History of. By C. A. FYFFE, M.A. Vol. I., from 1792 to 1814. 12s. Vol. II., from 1814 to 1848. 12s.
Music, Illustrated History of. By EMIL NAUMANN. Edited by the Rev. Sir F. A. GORE OUSELEY, Bart. Illustrated. Two Vols. 31s. 6d.
National Library, Cassell's. In Weekly Volumes, each containing about 192 pages. Paper covers, 3d.; cloth, 6d. (*A List sent post free on application.*)
Natural History, Cassell's Concise. By E. PERCEVAL WRIGHT, M.A., M.D., F.L.S. With several Hundred Illustrations. 7s. 6d.
Natural History, Cassell's New. Edited by Prof. P. MARTIN DUNCAN, M.B., F.R.S., F.G.S. With Contributions by Eminent Scientific Writers. Complete in Six Vols. With about 2,000 high-class Illustrations. Extra crown 4to, cloth, 9s. each.
Nature, Short Studies from. Illustrated. 5s.
Nimrod in the North; or, Hunting and Fishing Adventures in the Arctic Regions. By F. SCHWATKA. Illustrated. 7s. 6d.
Nursing for the Home and for the Hospital, A Handbook of. By CATHERINE J. WOOD. *Cheap Edition.* 1s. 6d.; cloth, 2s.
Oil Painting, A Manual of. By the Hon. JOHN COLLIER. 2s. 6d.
Our Homes, and How to Make them Healthy. By Eminent Authorities. Illustrated. 15s.; half-morocco, 21s.
Our Own Country. Six Vols. With 1,200 Illustrations. 7s. 6d. each.
Painting, Practical Guides to. With Coloured Plates and full instructions:—Animal Painting, 5s.—China Painting, 5s.—Figure Painting, 7s. 6d.—Flower Painting, 2 Books, 5s. each.—Tree Painting, 5s.—Water-Colour Painting, 5s.—Neutral Tint, 5s.—Sepia, in 2 Vols., 3s. each.—Flowers, and How to Paint Them, 5s.

Selections from Cassell & Company's Publications.

Paris, Cassell's Illustrated Guide to. 1s.; cloth, 2s.
Parliaments, A Diary of Two. By H. W. Lucy. The Disraeli Parliament, 1874—1880. 12s. The Gladstone Parliament, 1881—1886. 12s.
Paxton's Flower Garden. By Sir Joseph Paxton and Prof. Lindley. Three Vols. With 100 Coloured Plates. £1 1s. each.
Peoples of the World, The. In Six Vols. By Dr. Robert Brown. Illustrated. 7s. 6d. each.
Phantom City, The. By W. Westall. 5s.
Photography for Amateurs. By T. C. Hepworth. Illustrated. 1s.; or cloth, 1s. 6d.
Phrase and Fable, Dictionary of. By the Rev. Dr. Brewer. *Cheap Edition, Enlarged*, cloth, 3s. 6d.; or with leather back, 4s. 6d.
Picturesque America. Complete in Four Vols., with 48 Exquisite Steel Plates and about 800 Original Wood Engravings. £2 2s. each.
Picturesque Canada. With 600 Original Illustrations. Two Vols. £3 3s. each.
Picturesque Europe. Complete in Five Vols. Each containing 13 Exquisite Steel Plates, from Original Drawings, and nearly 200 Original Illustrations. £10 10s. The Popular Edition is published in Five Vols., 18s. each.
Pigeon Keeper, The Practical. By Lewis Wright. Illustrated. 3s. 6d.
Pigeons, The Book of. By Robert Fulton. Edited and Arranged by L. Wright. With 50 Coloured Plates, 31s. 6d.; half-morocco, £2 2s.
Poems and Pictures. With numerous Illustrations. 5s.
Poets, Cassell's Miniature Library of the :—

Burns. Two Vols. 2s. 6d.	Milton. Two Vols. 2s. 6d.
Byron. Two Vols. 2s. 6d.	Scott. Two Vols. 2s. 6d. [2s. 6d.
Hood. Two Vols. 2s. 6d.	Sheridan and Goldsmith. 2 Vols.
Longfellow. Two Vols. 2s. 6d.	Wordsworth. Two Vols. 2s. 6d.

Shakespeare. Twelve Vols., in Case, 15s.

*** *The above are also publishing in cloth, 1s. each Vol.*

Police Code, and Manual of the Criminal Law. By C. E. Howard Vincent, M.P. 2s.

Popular Library, Cassell's. Cloth, 1s. each.

The Russian Empire.	The Story of the English Jacobins.
The Religious Revolution in the 16th Century.	Domestic Folk Lore.
	The Rev. Rowland Hill: Preacher and Wit.
English Journalism.	Boswell and Johnson: their Companions and Contemporaries.
Our Colonial Empire.	
John Wesley.	The Scottish Covenanters.
The Young Man in the Battle of Life.	History of the Free-Trade Movement in England.

Poultry Keeper, The Practical. By L. Wright. With Coloured Plates and Illustrations. 3s. 6d.
Poultry, The Illustrated Book of. By L. Wright. With Fifty Coloured Plates. Cloth, 31s. 6d.; half-morocco, £2 2s.
Poultry, The Book of. By Lewis Wright. *Popular Edition.* 10s. 6d.
Quiver Yearly Volume, The. With about 300 Original Contributions by Eminent Divines and Popular Authors, and upwards of 250 high-class Illustrations. 7s. 6d.
Rabbit-Keeper, The Practical. By Cuniculus. Illustrated. 3s. 6d.

Selections from Cassell & Company's Publications.

Red Library, Cassell's. Stiff covers, 1s. each; cloth, 2s each: or half-calf, marbled edges, 5s. each.

Deerslayer.
Eugene Aram.
Jack Hinton, the Guardsman.
Rome and the Early Christians.
The Trials of Margaret Lyndsay.
Old Mortality.
The Hour and the Man.
Scarlet Letter.
Poe's Works.
Pride and Prejudice.
Last of the Mohicans.
Heart of Midlothian.
Last Days of Pompeii.

Yellowplush Papers.
Handy Andy.
Washington Irving's
Last Day of Palmyra.
Tales of the Borders.
American Humour.
Sketches by Boz.
Macaulay's Lays and Selected
Harry Lorrequer.
Old Curiosity Shop.
Rienzi.
The Talisman.
Pickwick (2 Vols.)

[Book-Sketch-
[Essays.

Representative Poems of Living Poets American and English. Selected by the Poets themselves. 15s.
Royal River, The: The Thames from Source to Sea. With Descriptive Text and a Series of beautiful Engravings. £2 2s.
Russia. By Sir DONALD MACKENZIE WALLACE, M.A. 5s.
Russo-Turkish War, Cassell's History of. With about 500 Illustrations. Two Vols., 9s. each.
Sandwith, Humphry. A Memoir by T. H. WARD. 7s. 6d.
Saturday Journal, Cassell's. Yearly Volume. 6s.
Science for All. Edited by Dr. ROBERT BROWN, M.A., F.L.S., &c. With 1,500 Illustrations. Five Vols. 9s. each.
Sea, The: Its Stirring Story of Adventure, Peril, and Heroism. By F. WHYMPER. With 400 Illustrations. Four Vols., 7s. 6d. each.
Sent Back by the Angels. And other Ballads. By FREDERICK LANGBRIDGE, M.A. Cloth, 4s. 6d.
Shaftesbury, The Seventh Earl of, K.G., The Life and Work of. By EDWIN HODDER. With Portraits. Three Vols., 36s.
Shakspere, The Leopold. With 400 Illustrations. Cloth, 6s.; cloth gilt, 7s. 6d.; half-morocco, 10s. 6d.
Shakspere, The Royal. With Steel Plates and Wood Engravings. Three Vols. 15s. each.
Shakespeare, Cassell's Quarto Edition. Edited by CHARLES and MARY COWDEN CLARKE, and containing about 600 Illustrations by H. C. SELOUS. Complete in Three Vols., cloth gilt, £3 3s.
Shakespeare's Romeo and Juliet. *Édition de Luxe.* Illustrated with Twelve Superb Photogravures from Original Drawings by F. DICKSEE, A.R.A. £5 5s.
Shakespearean Scenes and Characters. With 30 Steel Plates and 10 Wood Engravings. The Text written by AUSTIN BRERETON. 21s.
Sketching from Nature in Water Colours. By AARON PENLEY. With Illustrations in Chromo-Lithography. 15s.
Skin and Hair, The Management of the. By MALCOLM MORRIS, F.R.C.S. 2s.
Smith, The Adventures and Discourses of Captain John. By JOHN ASHTON. Illustrated. 5s.
Sports and Pastimes, Cassell's Book of. With more than 800 Illustrations and Coloured Frontispiece. 768 pages. 9s. (Can be had separately thus: Outdoor Sports, 7s. 6d.; Indoor Amusements, 3s. 6d.)
Steam Engine, The Theory and Action of the: for Practical Men. By W. H. NORTHCOTT, C.E. 3s. 6d.
Stock Exchange Year-Book, The. By THOMAS SKINNER. 10s. 6d.
Stones of London, The. By E. F. FLOWER. 6d.
"Stories from Cassell's." A Series of Seven Books. 6d. each; cloth lettered, 9d. each.
Sunlight and Shade. With numerous Exquisite Engravings. 7s. 6d.
Surgery, Memorials of the Craft of, in England. With an Introduction by Sir JAMES PAGET. 21s.

Selections from Cassell & Company's Publications.

Telegraph Guide, The. Illustrated. 1s.
Thackeray, Character Sketches from. Six New and Original Drawings by FREDERICK BARNARD, reproduced in Photogravure. 21s.
Trajan. An American Novel. By H. F. KEENAN. 7s. 6d.
Transformations of Insects, The. By Prof. P. MARTIN DUNCAN, M.B., F.R.S. With 240 Illustrations. 6s.
Treasure Island. By R. L. STEVENSON. Illustrated. 5s.
Treatment, The Year-Book of. A Critical Review for Practitioners of Medicine and Surgery. 5s.
Trees, Familiar. First Series. By G. S. BOULGER, F.L.S., F.G.S. With 40 full-page Coloured Plates, from Original Paintings by W. H. J. BOOT. 12s. 6d.
Twenty Photogravures of Pictures in the Salon of 1885, by the leading French Artists.
"Unicode": the Universal Telegraphic Phrase Book. 2s. 6d. each.
United States, Cassell's History of the. By EDMUND OLLIER. With 600 Illustrations. Three Vols. 9s. each.
Universal History, Cassell's Illustrated. Four Vols. 9s. each.
Vicar of Wakefield and other Works by OLIVER GOLDSMITH. Illustrated. 3s. 6d.; cloth, gilt edges, 5s.
Wealth-Creation. By AUGUSTUS MONGREDIEN. 5s.
Westall, W., Novels by. *Popular Editions.* Cloth, 2s. each.
RALPH NORBRECK'S TRUST.
THE OLD FACTORY. | RED RYVINGTON.
What Girls Can Do. By PHYLLIS BROWNE. 2s. 6d.
Wild Animals and Birds: their Haunts and Habits. By Dr. ANDREW WILSON. Illustrated. 7s. 6d.
Wild Birds, Familiar. First and Second Series. By W. SWAYSLAND. With 40 Coloured Plates in each. 12s. 6d. each.
Wild Flowers, Familiar. By F. E. HULME, F.L.S., F.S.A. Five Series. With 40 Coloured Plates in each. 12s. 6d. each.
Winter in India, A. By the Rt. Hon. W. E. BAXTER, M.P. 5s.
Wise Woman, The. By GEORGE MACDONALD. 2s. 6d.
Wood Magic: A Fable. By RICHARD JEFFERIES. 6s.
World of the Sea. Translated from the French of MOQUIN TANDON, by the Very Rev. H. MARTYN HART, M.A. Illustrated. Cloth. 6s.
World of Wit and Humour, The. With 400 Illustrations. Cloth, 7s. 6d.; cloth gilt, gilt edges, 10s. 6d.
World of Wonders. Two Vols. With 400 Illustrations. 7s. 6d. each.
Yule Tide. Cassell's Christmas Annual, 1s.

MAGAZINES.

The Quiver, for Sunday Reading. Monthly, 6d.
Cassell's Family Magazine. Monthly, 7d.
"Little Folks" Magazine. Monthly, 6d.
The Magazine of Art. Monthly, 1s.
The Lady's World. Monthly, 1s.
Cassell's Saturday Journal. Weekly, 1d.; Monthly, 6d.

Catalogues of CASSELL & COMPANY'S PUBLICATIONS, which may be had at all Booksellers', or will be sent post free on application to the publishers:—

CASSELL'S COMPLETE CATALOGUE, containing particulars of One Thousand Volumes.

CASSELL'S CLASSIFIED CATALOGUE, in which their Works are arranged according to price, from *Threepence to Twenty-five Guineas.*

CASSELL'S EDUCATIONAL CATALOGUE, containing particulars of CASSELL & COMPANY'S Educational Works and Students' Manuals.

CASSELL & COMPANY, LIMITED, *Ludgate Hill, London.*

Selections from Cassell & Company's Publications.

Bibles and Religious Works.

Bible, The Crown Illustrated. With about 1,000 Original Illustrations. With References, &c. 1,248 pages, crown 4to, cloth, 7s. 6d.
Bible, Cassell's Illustrated Family. With 900 Illustrations. Leather, gilt edges, £2 10s.
Bible Dictionary, Cassell's. With nearly 600 Illustrations. 7s. 6d.
Bible Educator, The. Edited by the Very Rev. Dean PLUMPTRE, D.D., Wells. With Illustrations, Maps, &c. Four Vols., cloth, 6s. each.
Bible Work at Home and Abroad. Volume. Illustrated. 3s.
Bunyan's Pilgrim's Progress (Cassell's Illustrated). Demy 4to. Illustrated throughout. 7s. 6d.
Bunyan's Pilgrim's Progress. With Illustrations. Cloth, 3s. 6d.
Child's Life of Christ, The. With 200 Illustrations. 21s.
Child's Bible, The. With 200 Illustrations. 143rd *Thousand.* 7s. 6d.
Church at Home, The. A Series of Short Sermons. By the Rt. Rev. ROWLEY HILL, D.D., Bishop of Sodor and Man. 5s.
Day-Dawn in Dark Places; or, Wanderings and Work in Bechwanaland. By the Rev. JOHN MACKENZIE. Illustrated. 3s. 6d.
Dictionary of Religion, The. An Encyclopædia of Christian and other Religious Doctrines, Denominations, Sects, Heresies, Ecclesiastical Terms, History, Biography, &c. &c. By the Rev. WILLIAM BENHAM, B.D. Cloth, 21s.; Roxburgh, 25s.
Doré Bible. With 230 Illustrations by GUSTAVE DORÉ. Cloth, £2 10s.
Early Days of Christianity, The. By the Ven. Archdeacon FARRAR, D.D., F.R.S.
  LIBRARY EDITION. Two Vols., 24s.; morocco, £2 2s.
  POPULAR EDITION. Complete in One Volume, cloth, 6s.; cloth, gilt edges, 7s. 6d.; Persian morocco, 10s. 6d.; tree-calf, 15s.
Family Prayer-Book, The. Edited by Rev. Canon GARBETT, M.A., and Rev. S. MARTIN. Extra crown 4to, cloth, 5s.; morocco, 18s.
Geikie, Cunningham, D.D., Works by:—
  HOURS WITH THE BIBLE. Six Vols., 6s. each.
  ENTERING ON LIFE. 3s. 6d.
  THE PRECIOUS PROMISES. 2s. 6d.
  THE ENGLISH REFORMATION. 5s.
  OLD TESTAMENT CHARACTERS. 6s.
  THE LIFE AND WORDS OF CHRIST. Two Vols., cloth, 30s. *Students'* Edition. Two Vols., 16s.
Glories of the Man of Sorrows, The. By Rev. H. G. BONAVIA HUNT, F.R.S., Ed.: Evening preacher at St. James's, Piccadilly. 2s. 6d.
Gospel of Grace, The. By a LINDESIE. Cloth, 3s. 6d.
"Heart Chords." A Series of Works by Eminent Divines. Bound in cloth, red edges, One Shilling each.

My Father.	My Aspirations.	My Hereafter.
My Bible.	My Emotional Life.	My Walk with God.
My Work for God.	My Body.	My Aids to the Divine Life.
My Object in Life.	My Soul.	My Sources of Strength.
	My Growth in Divine Life.	

Helps to Belief. A Series of Helpful Manuals on the Religious Difficulties of the Day. Edited by the Rev. TEIGNMOUTH SHORE, M.A., Chaplain-in-Ordinary to the Queen. Cloth, 1s. each.

CREATION. By the Lord Bishop of Carlisle.	MIRACLES. By the Rev. Brownlow Maitland, M.A.
THE DIVINITY OF OUR LORD. By the Lord Bishop of Derry.	PRAYER. By the Rev. T. Teignmouth Shore, M.A.
THE MORALITY OF THE OLD TESTAMENT. By the Rev. Newman Smyth, D.D.	THE RESURRECTION. By the Lord Archbishop of York.
	THE ATONEMENT. By the Lord Bishop of Peterborough.

Lay Texts for the Young. In English and French. By Mrs. RICHARD STRACHEY. 2s. 6d.

Selections from Cassell & Company's Publications.

Life of Christ, The. By the Ven. Archdeacon FARRAR, D.D., F.R.S.
   ILLUSTRATED EDITION, with about 300 Original Illustrations. Extra crown 4to, cloth, gilt edges, 21s.; morocco antique, 42s.
   LIBRARY EDITION. Two Vols. Cloth, 24s.; morocco, 42s.
   BIJOU EDITION. Five Volumes, in box, 10s. 6d. the set.
   POPULAR EDITION, in One Vol. 8vo, cloth, 6s.; cloth, gilt edges, 7s. 6d.; Persian morocco, gilt edges, 10s. 6d.; tree calf, 15s.

Marriage Ring, The. By WILLIAM LANDELS, D.D. Bound in white leatherette, gilt edges, in box, 6s.; morocco, 8s. 6d.

Moses and Geology; or, The Harmony of the Bible with Science. By the Rev. SAMUEL KINNS, Ph.D., F.R.A.S. Illustrated. *Cheap Edition*, 6s.

Music of the Bible, The. By J. STAINER, M.A., Mus. Doc. 2s. 6d.

New Testament Commentary for English Readers, The. Edited by the Rt. Rev. C. J. ELLICOTT, D.D., Lord Bishop of Gloucester and Bristol. In Three Volumes, 21s. each.
   Vol. I.—The Four Gospels.
   Vol. II.—The Acts, Romans, Corinthians, Galatians.
   Vol. III.—The remaining Books of the New Testament.

Old Testament Commentary for English Readers, The. Edited by the Right Rev. C. J. ELLICOTT, D.D., Lord Bishop of Gloucester and Bristol. Complete in 5 Vols., 21s. each.
   Vol. I.—Genesis to Numbers.
   Vol. II.—Deuteronomy to Samuel II.
   Vol. III.—Kings I. to Esther.
   Vol. IV.—Job to Isaiah.
   Vol. V.—Jeremiah to Malachi.

Patriarchs, The. By the late Rev. W. HANNA, D.D., and the Ven. Archdeacon NORRIS, B.D. 2s. 6d.

Protestantism, The History of. By the Rev. J. A. WYLIE, LL.D. Containing upwards of 600 Original Illustrations. Three Vols., 27s.

Quiver Yearly Volume, The. 250 high-class Illustrations. 7s. 6d.

Revised Version—Commentary on the Revised Version of the New Testament. By the Rev. W. G. HUMPHRY, B.D. 7s. 6d.

Sacred Poems, The Book of. Edited by the Rev. Canon BAYNES, M.A. With Illustrations. Cloth, gilt edges, 5s.

St. George for England; and other Sermons preached to Children. By the Rev. T. TEIGNMOUTH SHORE, M.A. 5s.

St. Paul, The Life and Work of. By the Ven. Archdeacon FARRAR, D.D., F.R.S., Chaplain-in-Ordinary to the Queen.
   LIBRARY EDITION. Two Vols., cloth, 24s.; morocco, 42s.
   ILLUSTRATED EDITION, complete in One Volume, with about 300 Illustrations, £1 1s.; morocco, £2 2s.
   POPULAR EDITION. One Volume, 8vo, cloth, 6s.; cloth, gilt edges, 7s. 6d.; Persian morocco, 10s. 6d.; tree calf, 15s.

Secular Life, The Gospel of the. Sermons preached at Oxford. By the Hon. W. H. FREMANTLE, Canon of Canterbury. 5s.

Sermons Preached at Westminster Abbey. By ALFRED BARRY, D.D., D.C.L., Primate of Australia. 5s.

Shall We Know One Another? By the Rt. Rev. J. C RYLE, D.D., Bishop of Liverpool. *New and Enlarged Edition*. Cloth limp, 1s.

Simon Peter: His Life, Times, and Friends. By E. HODDER. 5s.

Twilight of Life, The. Words of Counsel and Comfort for the Aged. By the Rev. JOHN ELLERTON, M.A. 1s. 6d.

Voice of Time, The. By JOHN STROUD. Cloth gilt, 1s.

Selections from Cassell & Company's Publications.

Educational Works and Students' Manuals.

Alphabet, Cassell's Pictorial. 3s. 6d.
Algebra, The Elements of. By Prof. WALLACE, M.A. 1s.
Arithmetics, The Modern School. By GEORGE RICKS, B.Sc. Lond. With Test Cards. (*List on application.*)
Book-Keeping. By THEODORE JONES. For Schools, 2s.; cloth, 3s. For the Million, 2s.; cloth, 3s. Books for Jones's System. 2s.
Chemistry, The Public School. By J. H. ANDERSON, M.A. 2s. 6d.
Commentary, The New Testament. Edited by the Lord Bishop of GLOUCESTER and BRISTOL. Handy Volume Edition.
St. Matthew, 3s. 6d. St. Mark, 3s. St. Luke, 3s. 6d. St. John, 3s. 6d. The Acts of the Apostles, 3s. 6d. Romans, 2s. 6d. Corinthians I. and II., 3s. Galatians, Ephesians, and Philippians, 3s. Colossians, Thessalonians, and Timothy, 3s. Titus, Philemon, Hebrews, and James, 3s. Peter, Jude, and John, 3s. The Revelation, 3s. An Introduction to the New Testament, 3s. 6d.
Commentary, Old Testament. Edited by Bishop ELLICOTT. Handy Volume Edition. Genesis, 3s. 6d. Exodus, 3s. Leviticus, 3s. Numbers, 2s. 6d. Deuteronomy, 2s. 6d.
Copy-Books, Cassell's Graduated. *Eighteen Books.* 2d. each.
Copy-Books, The Modern School. *Twelve Books.* 2d. each.
Drawing Books, Cassell's New Standard. 7 Books. 2d. each.
Drawing Books, Superior. 4 Books. Price 5s. each.
Drawing Copies, Cassell's Modern School Freehand. First Grade, 1s.; Second Grade, 2s.
Drawing Copies, Cassell's New Standard. Seven Books. 2d. each.
Electricity, Practical. By Prof. W. E. AYRTON. 7s. 6d.
Energy and Motion: A Text-Book of Elementary Mechanics. By WILLIAM PAICE, M.A. Illustrated. 1s. 6d.
English Literature, First Sketch of. *New and Enlarged Edition.* By Prof. MORLEY. 7s. 6d.
Euclid, Cassell's. Edited by Prof. WALLACE, M.A. 1s.
Euclid, The First Four Books of. In paper, 6d.; cloth, 9d.
French Reader, Cassell's Public School. By GUILLAUME S. CONRAD. 2s. 6d.
French, Cassell's Lessons in. *New and Revised Edition.* Parts I. and II., each 2s. 6d.; complete, 4s. 6d. Key, 1s. 6d.
French-English and English-French Dictionary. *Entirely New and Enlarged Edition.* 1,150 pages, 8vo, cloth, 3s. 6d.
Galbraith and Haughton's Scientific Manuals. By the Rev. Prof. GALBRAITH, M.A., and the Rev. Prof. HAUGHTON, M.D., D.C.L. Arithmetic, 3s. 6d.—Plane Trigonometry, 2s. 6d.—Euclid, Books I., II., III., 2s. 6d.—Books IV., V., VI., 2s. 6d.—Mathematical Tables, 3s. 6d.—Mechanics, 3s. 6d.—Optics, 2s. 6d.—Hydrostatics, 3s. 6d.—Astronomy, 5s.—Steam Engine, 3s. 6d.—Algebra, Part I., cloth, 2s. 6d.; Complete, 7s. 6d.—Tides and Tidal Currents, with Tidal Cards, 3s.
Geometry, Practical Solid. By Major ROSS, R.E. 2s.
German-English and English-German Dictionary. *Entirely New and Revised Edition.* 3s. 6d.
German Reading, First Lessons in. By A. JAGST. Illustrated. 1s.
German of To-Day. By Dr. HEINEMANN. 1s. 6d.
Handbook of New Code of Regulations. By JOHN F. MOSS. 1s.
Historical Course for Schools, Cassell's. Illustrated throughout.
I.—Stories from English History, 1s. II.—The Simple Outline of English History, 1s. 3d. III.—The Class History of England, 2s. 6d.
Latin-English Dictionary, Cassell's. By J. R. V. MARCHANT, M.A. 3s. 6d.

Selections from Cassell & Company's Publications.

Latin-English and English-Latin Dictionary. By J. R. BEARD, D.D., and C. BEARD, B.A. Crown 8vo, 914 pp., 3s. 6d.
Little Folks' History of England. By ISA CRAIG-KNOX. With 30 Illustrations. 1s. 6d.
Making of the Home, The: A Book of Domestic Economy for School and Home Use. By Mrs. SAMUEL A. BARNETT. 1s. 6d.
Marlborough Books:—Arithmetic Examples, 3s. Arithmetic Rules, 1s. 6d. French Exercises, 3s. 6d. French Grammar, 2s. 6d. German Grammar, 3s. 6d.
Music, An Elementary Manual of. By HENRY LESLIE. 1s.
Natural Philosophy. By Prof. HAUGHTON, F.R.S. Illustrated. 3s. 6d.
Popular Educator, Cassell's. *New and Thoroughly Revised Edition.* Illustrated throughout. Complete in Six Vols., 5s. each.
Physical Science, Intermediate Text-Book of. By F. H. BOWMAN, D.Sc., F.R.A.S., F.L.S. Illustrated. 3s. 6d.
Readers, Cassell's Readable. Carefully graduated, extremely interesting, and illustrated throughout. (*List on application.*)
Readers, Cassell's Historical. Illustrated throughout, printed on superior paper, and strongly bound in cloth. (*List on application.*)
Readers for Infant Schools, Coloured. Three Books. Each containing 48 pages, including 8 pages in colours. 4d. each.
Reader, The Citizen. By H. O. ARNOLD-FORSTER, with Preface by the late Right Hon. W. E. FORSTER, M.P. 1s. 6d.
Readers, The Modern Geographical, illustrated throughout, and strongly bound in cloth. (*List on application.*)
Readers, The Modern School. Illustrated. (*List on application.*)
Reading and Spelling Book, Cassell's Illustrated. 1s.
Right Lines; or, Form and Colour. With Illustrations. 1s.
School Bank Manual. By AGNES LAMBERT. Price 6d.
School Manager's Manual. By F. C. MILLS, M.A. 1s.
Shakspere's Plays for School Use. 5 Books. Illustrated, 6d. each.
Shakspere Reading Book, The. By H. COURTHOPE BOWEN, M.A. Illustrated. 3s. 6d. Also issued in Three Books, 1s. each.
Spelling, A Complete Manual of. By J. D. MORELL, LL.D. 1s.
Technical Manuals, Cassell's. Illustrated throughout:—
Handrailing and Staircasing, 3s. 6d.—Bricklayers, Drawing for, 3s.—Building Construction, 2s.—Cabinet-Makers, Drawing for, 3s.—Carpenters and Joiners, Drawing for, 3s. 6d.—Gothic Stonework, 3s.—Linear Drawing and Practical Geometry, 2s.—Linear Drawing and Projection. The Two Vols. in One, 3s. 6d.—Machinists and Engineers, Drawing for, 4s. 6d.—Metal-Plate Workers, Drawing for, 3s.—Model Drawing, 3s.—Orthographical and Isometrical Projection, 2s.—Practical Perspective, 3s.—Stonemasons, Drawing for, 3s.—Applied Mechanics, by Sir R. S. Ball, LL.D., 2s.—Systematic Drawing and Shading, 2s.
Technical Educator, Cassell's. Four Vols. 6s. each. *New and Cheap Edition,* in Four Vols., 5s. each.
Technology, Manuals of. Edited by Prof. AYRTON, F.R.S., and RICHARD WORMELL, D.Sc., M.A. Illustrated throughout:—
The Dyeing of Textile Fabrics, by Prof. Hummel, 5s.—Watch and Clock Making, by D. Glasgow, 4s. 6d.—Steel and Iron, by W. H. Greenwood, F.C.S., Assoc. M.I.C.E., &c., 5s.—Spinning Woollen and Worsted, by W. S. Bright McLaren, 4s. 6d.—Design in Textile Fabrics, by T. R. Ashenhurst, 4s. 6d.—Practical Mechanics, by Prof. Perry, M.E., 3s. 6d.—Cutting Tools Worked by Hand and Machine, by Prof. Smith, 3s. 6d. *A Prospectus on application.*
Test Cards, Cassell's Combination. In sets, 1s. each.

CASSELL & COMPANY, LIMITED, *Ludgate Hill, London.*

Selections from Cassell & Company's Publications.

Books for Young People.

Books for Young People. Illustrated. Cloth gilt, 5s. each.

- **Under Bayard's Banner.** By Henry Frith.
- **The King's Command: A Story for Girls.** By Maggie Symington.
- **For Fortune and Glory; a Story of the Soudan War.** By Lewis Hough.
- **The Tales of the Sixty Mandarins.** By P. V. Ramaswami Raju. With an Introduction by Prof. Henry Morley.
- **"Follow My Leader;" or, the Boys of Templeton.** By Talbot Baines Reed.
- **The Romance of Invention.** By James Burnley.
- **The Champion of Odin; or, Viking Life in the Days of Old.** By J. Fred. Hodgetts.
- **Bound by a Spell; or, the Hunted Witch of the Forest.** By the Hon. Mrs. Greene.

Books for Young People. Illustrated. Price 3s. 6d. each.

- **A World of Girls: The Story of a School.** By L. T. Meade.
- **Lost among White Africans: A Boy's Adventures on the Upper Congo.** By David Ker.
- **Freedom's Sword: A Story of the Days of Wallace and Bruce.** By Annie S. Swan.
- **On Board the "Esmeralda;" or, Martin Leigh's Log.** By John C. Hutcheson.
- **In Quest of Gold: or, Under the Whanga Falls.** By Alfred St. Johnston.
- **For Queen and King; or, the Loyal 'Prentice.** By Henry Frith.

Perils Afloat and Brigands Ashore. By Alfred Elwes.

The "Cross and Crown" Series. Consisting of Stories founded on incidents which occurred during Religious Persecutions of Past Days. With Illustrations in each Book, printed on a tint. 2s. 6d. each.

- **Strong to Suffer: A Story of the Jews.** By E. Wynne.
- **Heroes of the Indian Empire; or, Stories of Valour and Victory.** By Ernest Foster.
- **In Letters of Flame: A Story of the Waldenses.** By C. L. Matéaux.
- **Through Trial to Triumph.** By Madeline B. Hunt.
- **By Fire and Sword: A Story of the Huguenots.** By Thomas Archer.
- **Adam Hepburn's Vow: A Tale of Kirk and Covenant.** By Annie S Swan.
- **No. XIII.; or, The Story of the Lost Vestal.** A Tale of Early Christian Days. By Emma Marshall.

The "Log Cabin" Series. By EDWARD S. ELLIS. With Four Full-age Illustrations in each. Crown 8vo, cloth, 2s. 6d. each.

The Lost Trail. | Camp-Fire and Wigwam. | Footprints in the Forest.

The "Great River" Series (uniform with the "Log Cabin" Series). By EDWARD S. ELLIS. Illustrated. Crown 8vo, cloth, bevelled boards, 2s. 6d. each.

Down the Mississippi. | Lost in the Wilds.
Up the Tapajos; or, Adventures in Brazil.

The "Boy Pioneer" Series. By EDWARD S. ELLIS. With Four Full-page Illustrations in each Book. Crown 8vo, cloth, 2s. 6d. each.

- **Ned in the Woods.** A Tale of Early Days in the West.
- **Ned on the River.** A Tale of Indian River Warfare.

Ned in the Block House. A Story of Pioneer Life in Kentucky.

"Golden Mottoes" Series, The. Each Book containing 208 pages, with Four full-page Original Illustrations. Crown 8vo, cloth gilt, 2s. each.

- **"Nil Desperandum."** By the Rev. F. Langbridge.
- **"Bear and Forbear."** By Sarah Pitt.
- **"Foremost if I Can."** By Helen Atteridge.
- **"Honour is my Guide."** By Jeanie Hering (Mrs. Adams-Acton).
- **"Aim at the Sure End."** By Emilie Searchfield.
- **"He Conquers who Endures."** By the Author of "May Cunningham's Trial," &c.

Selections from Cassell & Company's Publications.

Sunday School Reward Books. By Popular Authors. With Four Original Illustrations in each. Cloth gilt, 1s. 6d. each.

Rhoda's Reward; or, "If Wishes were Horses."
Jack Marston's Anchor.
Frank's Life-Battle; or, The Three Friends.
Rags and Rainbows: a Story of Thanksgiving.
Uncle William's Charges; or, The Broken Trust.
Pretty Pink's Purpose; or, The Little Street Merchants.

The New Children's Album. Fcap. 4to, 320 pages. Illustrated throughout. 3s. 6d.

The History Scrap Book. With nearly 1,000 Engravings. 5s.; cloth, 7s. 6d.

"Little Folks" Half-Yearly Volume. With 200 Illustrations and several Pictures in Colour. 3s. 6d.; or cloth gilt, 5s.

The Merry-go-Round. Original Poems for Children. Illustrated throughout. 5s.

Bo-Peep. A Book for the Little Ones. With Original Stories and Verses, Illustrated throughout. Boards, 2s. 6d.; cloth gilt, 3s. 6d.

The World's Lumber Room. By SELINA GAYE. Illustrated. 3s. 6d.

The "Proverbs" Series. Original Stories by Popular Authors, founded on and illustrating well-known Proverbs. With Four Illustrations in each Book, printed on a tint. 1s. 6d. each.

Fritters. By Sarah Pitt.
Trixy. By Maggie Symington.
The Two Hardcastles. By Madeline Bonavia Hunt.
Major Monk's Motto. By the Rev. F. Langbridge.
Tim Thomson's Trial. By George Weatherly.
Ursula's Stumbling-Block. By Julia Goddard.
Ruth's Life-Work. By the Rev. Joseph Johnson.

The World's Workers. A Series of New and Original Volumes. With Portraits printed on a tint as Frontispiece. 1s. each.

General Gordon. By the Rev. S. A. Swaine.
Charles Dickens. By his Eldest Daughter.
Sir Titus Salt and George Moore. By J. Burnley.
Florence Nightingale, Catherine Marsh, Frances Ridley Havergal, Mrs. Ranyard ("L.N.R."). By Lizzie Alldridge.
Dr. Guthrie, Father Mathew, Elihu Burritt, George Livesey. By the Rev. J. W. Kirton.
David Livingstone. By Robert Smiles.
Sir Henry Havelock and Colin Campbell, Lord Clyde. By E. C. Phillips.
Abraham Lincoln. By Ernest Foster.
George Müller and Andrew Reed. By E. R. Pitman.
Richard Cobden. By R. Gowing.
Benjamin Franklin. By E. M. Tomkinson.
Handel. By Eliza Clarke.
Turner the Artist. By the Rev. S. A. Swaine.
George and Robert Stephenson. By C. L. Matéaux.

The "Chimes" Series. Each containing 64 pages, with Illustrations on every page, and bound in Japanese morocco, 1s.

Bible Chimes.
Daily Chimes.
Holy Chimes.
Old World Chimes.

Sixpenny Story Books. All Illustrated, and containing Interesting Stories by well-known Writers.

Little Content.
The Smuggler's Cave.
Little Lizzie.
Little Bird.
The Boot on the Wrong Foot.
Luke Barnicott.
Little Pickles.
The Boat Club. By Oliver Optic.
Helpful Nellie; and other Stories.
The Elchester College Boys.
My First Cruise.
Lottie's White Frock.
Only Just Once.
The Little Peacemaker.
The Delft Jug. By Silverpen.

The "Baby's Album" Series. Four Books, each containing about 50 Illustrations. Price 6d. each; or cloth gilt, 1s. each.

Baby's Album.
Dolly's Album.
Fairy's Album.
Pussy's Album.

Selections from Cassell & Company's Publications.

Illustrated Books for the Little Ones. Containing interesting Stories. All Illustrated. 1s. each.

Indoors and Out.
Some Farm Friends.
Those Golden Sands.
Little Mothers & their Children.

Our Pretty Pets.
Our Schoolday Hours.
Creatures Tame.
Creatures Wild.

Shilling Story Books. All Illustrated, and containing Interesting Stories.

Thorns and Tangles.
The Cuckoo in the Robin's Nest.
John's Mistake.
The History of Five Little Pitchers.
Diamonds in the Sand.
Surly Bob.
The Giant's Cradle.

Shag and Doll.
Aunt Lucia's Locket.
The Magic Mirror.
The Cost of Revenge.
Clever Frank.
Among the Redskins.
The Ferryman of Br.ll.
Harry Maxwell.
A Banished Monarch.

" Little Folks " Painting Books. With Text, and Outline Illustrations for Water-Colour Painting. 1s. each.

Fruits and Blossoms for "Little Folks" to Paint.
The "Little Folks" Proverb Painting Book.
The "Little Folks" Illuminating Book.

Pictures to Paint.
"Little Folks" Painting Book.
"Litt.e Folks" Nature Painting Book.
Another "Little Folks" Painting Book.

Eighteenpenny Story Books. All Illustrated throughout.

Wee Little Rhymes.
Little One's Welcome.
Little Gossips.
Ding Dong Bell.
Three Wee Ulster Lassies.
Little Queen Mab.
Up the Ladder.
Dick's Hero; and other Stories.
The Chip Boy.
Raggles, Baggles, and the Emperor.

Roses from Thorns.
Faith's Father.
By Land and Sea.
The Young Berringtons.
Jeff and Left.
Tom Morris's Error.
Worth more than Gold.
"Through Flood—Through Fire;" and other Stories.
The Girl with the Golden Locks.
Stories of the Olden Time.

The " Cosy Corner " Series. Story Books for Children. Each containing nearly ONE HUNDRED PICTURES. 1s. 6d. each.

See-Saw Stories.
Little Chimes for All Times.
Wee Willie Winkie.
Pet's Posy of Pictures and Stor.es.
Dot's Story Book.

Story Flowers for Rainy Hours.
Little Talks with Little People.
Chats for Small Chatterers.
Pictures for Happy Hours.
Ups and Downs of a Donkey's Life.

The " World in Pictures." Illustrated throughout. 2s. 6d. each.

A Ramble Round France.
All the Russias.
Chats about Germany.
The Land of the Pyramids (Egypt).
Peeps into China.

The Eastern Wonderland (Japan).
Glimpses of South America.
Round Africa.
The Land of Temples (India).
The Isles of the Pacific.

Two-Shilling Story Books. All Illustrated.

Clover Blossoms.
Christmas Dreams.
Stories of the Tower.
Mr. Burke's Nieces.
May Cunningham's Trial.
The Top of the Ladder: How to Reach it.
Little Flotsam.
Madge and her Friends.
The Children of the Court.
A Moonbeam Tangle.

Maid Marjory.
The Four Cats of the Tippertons.
Marion's Two Homes.
Little Folks' Sunday Book.
Two Fourpenny Bits.
Poor Nelly.
Tom Heriot.
Through Peril to Fortune.
Aunt Tabitha's Waifs.
In Mischief Again.

Selections from Cassell & Company's Publications.

Half-Crown Story Books.

Arm-Chair Stories.
Little Hinges.
Margaret's Enemy.
Ken's Perplexities.
Notable Shipwrecks.
Golden Days.
Wonders of Common Things.
Little Empress Joan.
Truth will Out.
At the South Pole. *Cheap Edition.*
Soldier and Patriot (George Washington).
Picture of School Life and Boyhood.
The Young Man in the Battle of Life. By the Rev. Dr. Landels.
The True Glory of Woman. By the Rev. Dr. Landels.

Library of Wonders. Illustrated Gift-books for Boys. 2s. 6d. each.

Wonderful Adventures.
Wonders of Animal Instinct.
Wonders of Architecture.
Wonders of Acoustics.
Wonders of Water.
Wonderful Escapes.
Bodily Strength and Skill.
Wonderful Balloon Ascents.

Three and Sixpenny Library of Standard Tales, &c. All Illustrated and bound in cloth gilt. Crown 8vo. 3s. 6d. each.

Jane Austen and her Works.
Mission Life in Greece and Palestine.
The Dingy House at Kensington.
The Romance of Trade.
The Three Homes.
School Girls.
Deepdale Vicarage.
In Duty Bound.
The Half Sisters.
Peggy Oglivie's Inheritance.
The Family Honour.
Esther West.
Working to Win.
Krilof and his Fables. By W. R. S. Ralston, M.A.
Fairy Tales. By Prof. Morley.

The Home Chat Series. All Illustrated throughout. Fcap. 4to. Boards, 3s. 6d. each. Cloth, gilt edges, 5s. each.

Half-Hours with Early Explorers.
Stories about Animals.
Stories about Birds.
Paws and Claws.
Home Chat.
Peeps Abroad for Folks at Home.
Around and About Old England.

Books for the Little Ones.

Rhymes for the Young Folk. By William Allingham. Beautifully Illustrated. 3s. 6d.
The Little Doings of some Little Folks. By Chatty Cheerful. Illustrated. 5s.
The Sunday Scrap Book. With One Thousand Scripture Pictures. Boards, 5s.; cloth, 7s. 6d.
Daisy Dimple's Scrap Book. Containing about 1,000 Pictures. Boards, 5s.; cloth gilt, 7s. 6d.
Little Folks' Picture Album. With 168 Large Pictures. 5s.
Little Folks' Picture Gallery. With 150 Illustrations. 5s.
The Old Fairy Tales. With Original Illustrations. Boards, 1s.; cloth, 1s. 6d.
My Diary. With 12 Coloured Plates and 366 Woodcuts. 1s.
The Story of Robin Hood. With Coloured Illustrations. 2s. 6d.
The Pilgrim's Progress. With Coloured Illustrations. 2s. 6d.
Wee Little Rhymes. 1s. 6d.
Little One's Welcome. 1s. 6d.
Little Gossips. 1s. 6d.
Ding Dong Bell. 1s. 6d.
Clover Blossoms. 2s.
Christmas Dreams. 2s.
Arm-Chair Stories. 2s. 6d.

Books for Boys.

Captain Trafalgar: A Story of the Mexican Gulf. By W. Westall. Illustrated. 5s.
Kidnapped. By R. L. Stevenson. 5s.
King Solomon's Mines. By H. Rider Haggard. 5s.
The Phantom City. By W. Westall. 5s.
Treasure Island. By R. L. Stevenson. Illustrated. 5s.
Modern Explorers. By Thomas Frost. Illustrated. 5s.
Famous Sailors of Former Times. By Clements Markham. Illustrated. 2s. 6d.
Wild Adventures in Wild Places. By Dr. Gordon Stables, M.D., R.N. Illustrated. 5s.
Jungle, Peak, and Plain. By Dr. Gordon Stables, R.N. Illustrated. 5s.

CASSELL & COMPANY, Limited, London; Paris, New York & Melbourne.

www.ingramcontent.com/pod-product-compliance
Lightning Source LLC
Chambersburg PA
CBHW021730220426
43662CB00008B/774